Being Still

To Father Seraphim of Mount Athos

Being Still

Reflections on an Ancient Mystical Tradition

JEAN-YVES LELOUP

Translated and edited by M. S. Laird

GRACEWING

PAULIST PRESS
New York/Mahwah, N.J.

This work was first published in French in 1990 under the title *Écrits sur l'Hésychasme* by Editions Albin Michel S.A., 22, rue Huyghens, 75014 Paris.

First published in English in 2003
jointly by

Gracewing
2 Southern Avenue
Leominster
Herefordshire
HR6 0QF
www.gracewing.co.uk

Paulist Press
997 Macarthur Boulevard
Mahwah
New Jersey 07430
USA
www.paulistpress.com

The right of Jean-Yves Leloup to be identified as the author of this work has been asserted in accordance with the Copyright, Designs and Patents Act 1988.

UK ISBN 0 85244 537 7
US ISBN 0-8091-4177-9

Library of Congress Cataloging-in-Publication Data

Leloup, Jean-Yves.
  [Ecrits sur l'hâesychasme. English]
  Being still : reflections on a forgotten mystical tradition / Jean-Yves Leloup ; translated and edited by M.S. Laird.
     p. cm.
  ISBN 0-8091-4177-9
  1. Hesychasm. 2. Mysticism--Orthodox Eastern Church. I. Title.
  BX384.5 .L4513 2003
  248.4'819--dc21

                            2002012213

Typeset by Action Publishing Technology Ltd,
Gloucester GL1 5SR

Printed in England by
MPG Books Ltd,
Bodmin PL31 1EG

Contents

TRANSLATOR'S NOTE: All direct quotations from Scripture are from the New Jerusalem Bible. Indirect quotations and paraphrases are translated from the author's French. The translator wishes to thank the reader from Gracewing for many helpful editorial suggestions.

Introduction

Heavy sun. It must be about noon. The path continues its ascent. In spite of hunger and fatigue I'll continue – besides, where could I possibly sit down? On one side of me is a sheer cliff, on the other, the steep face of the mountain. Kapsokalivià is one of the steepest and most arid places on Mount Athos. Someone had told me, 'Over there you will find hermits. Most of them will be mad, or filthy or ignorant, but it's worth the effort.' I replied that I had not come to Mount Athos to see zoo animals on the verge of extinction. But now I ask myself what am I doing here on this rocky path which seems to lead nowhere? Mere curiosity? The desire to see God in the flesh rather than in the pages of a book? I glimpsed a hut with some garden in front. A monk is standing there with a rosary, made of knotted wool, in his hand. I expect to see some gesture of retreat or alarm as I approach, but instead the monk smiles and raises his finger to his mouth, indicating that I should remain silent. There is something strange about his gaze. I can't tell the colour of his eyes; they are bottomless. Suddenly I feel light-headed and he motions me to sit down. Then he disappears down a track, leaving me rather perplexed, facing the sea, facing my thoughts ...

Ninety minutes pass. Irritated by the wait, and somewhat anxious, I see him reappear, carrying a pot of jam and some water. It dawns on me that he has been walking all this time, in the scorching sun, just to quench my thirst!

As he hands me the pot of jam, I get a better look at his eyes, two extraordinary abysses of water and light. Love is not quite the word, but it will suffice. I begin to drink and feel for a moment I will never thirst again.

The smallest act of pure love seems bigger than the grandest cathedral. That day I entered Christianity by its main portal, a pot of jam, the Infinite in a routine gesture.

For years now this anonymous figure, always silent, has never ceased to smile at me: a splinter of water and light in the burnt flesh of my story.

Kapsokalivià
Mount Athos
24 June 1969

Chapter One

The Way of Hesychastic Prayer According to Father Seraphim

When Mr. X, a young French philosopher, arrived on Mount Athos, he had already read a number of books on Orthodox spirituality, including *Writings from the Philokalia on Prayer of the Heart* and *The Way of a Pilgrim*. He had been seduced without really being convinced. A single liturgy at rue Daru in Paris had inspired him to spend a few days on Mount Athos when he was on holiday in Greece. He hoped to learn a bit more about prayer and, in particular, the method of prayer practised by those silent men in search of *hesychasm*, or interior peace. This young man had read many books on meditation and prayer, but he had never really prayed or meditated before. He was looking for not one more lecture on prayer or meditation, but an initiation which would allow him to *live* prayer and *to know* it from within, by experience and not just by hearsay.

It would take too long to tell how he came to meet Fr. Seraphim, a monk who lived in a hermitage near Saint Panteleimon (which the Greeks call the Roussikon). Suffice it to say that on Mount Athos the young philosopher was a little wary. He did not find the monks up to the level of his books.

Fr. Seraphim had an ambiguous reputation among his

circle of monks. Some accused him of levitating, others of barking. Some considered him an ignorant peasant, others a true staretz, inspired by the Holy Spirit and capable of giving profound advice and reading the secrets of the heart.

When anyone arrived at the door of his hermitage, Fr. Seraphim had the custom of observing the visitor in a most insolent way from head to foot, for five long minutes, without saying a word. Those who were not put off by this sort of examination would then undergo the monk's biting evaluation. 'You! He hasn't descended beneath your chin.' 'You! Let's not talk about it, He hasn't even come into you.' 'You! How marvellous! He's got right down to your knees!'

Of course he was speaking of the Holy Spirit's descent. In this way, he assessed the holiness of a visitor according to the degree of incarnation of the Spirit. The perfect person, the transfigured person, was inhabited by the Holy Spirit from head to toe. 'I've only seen that once. That was staretz Silouan. He was truly a man of God, full of humility and majesty.'

The young philosopher was not quite there yet. The Holy Spirit had stopped at his chin. When he asked Fr. Seraphim to tell him something about prayer of the heart and about pure prayer according to Evagrius Ponticus, the old monk began to shout. This did not discourage the young man. He insisted. So Fr. Seraphim said, 'Before I talk about prayer of the heart, first learn how to meditate like a mountain.' And he showed him an enormous rock. 'Ask it how it goes about praying. Then come back to me.'

To Meditate like a Mountain

Thus began the young philosopher's true initiation into the way of silent prayer. His first instructions concerned stability: settling into a good posture. Indeed the first counsel to give anyone who wants to meditate is not on the spiritual level but on the *physical*. Sit down.

To sit like a mountain also means to feel your weight, to be heavy with presence. For the first few days, the young man had great difficulty remaining so stationary, with legs crossed, and the hips a little above the knees: it was in this posture that he found the most stability. One morning he really felt what it meant 'to meditate like a mountain'. He was there with all his weight. One with the mountain, silent under the sun. His understanding of time had changed completely. Mountains know another time, another rhythm. To be seated like a mountain is to have eternity before you. It's the right attitude for anyone who wants to enter into meditation. It is to know you have eternity behind, within and before you. Before building a church there has to be rock. On the unshakeable foundation of rock God could build the Church and make the human body his temple. 'You are Peter, the rock, and on this rock I shall build my Church.'

The young man stayed this way for several weeks. The hardest thing for him was to spend hours like this doing nothing. He had to learn once again how to be, simply to be, without aim or purpose. To meditate like a mountain was the true meditation of being, before all thought, pleasure and pain.

Fr. Seraphim visited him every day and shared his tomatoes and a few olives. Despite this rather frugal regime, the young man seemed to have put on weight. He walked with greater calm. The mountain had become part of him. He knew how to take his time, to greet the seasons, to keep silent and calm like earth, at times hard and dry, but also like a hillside awaiting the harvest.

Meditating like a mountain modified the rhythm of his thoughts. He learnt to see without judging, as though he were giving to all that grows on the mountain the right to exist.

One day some pilgrims, impressed by the quality of his presence, took him for a monk and asked his blessing. He said nothing, imperturbable as a rock. When Fr. Seraphim learnt of this he began that very evening to beat him black and blue. The young man began to groan.

'Good,' said the old monk, 'I thought you'd become as stupid as the stones on the road. Silent prayer puts down roots. It has the stability of mountains, but its purpose is not to make you a dead branch, but someone alive.'

He took the young man by the arm and led him to the bottom of the garden where there were a few flowers amongst the wild herbs.

'Now you must learn how to meditate like a poppy, but don't forget about the mountain.'

To Meditate like a Poppy

Thus the young man began to flower.

Meditation is first of all a posture, and this is what the mountain had taught him. Meditation is also a certain orientation, and this is what the poppy was going to teach him: to turn towards the sun, to turn from the depths of himself towards the light, to make of meditation the aspiration of all his strength and vigour.

This turning towards beauty, towards the light caused him at times to grow red like a poppy, as if the beautiful light were that of a face that smiled on him and expected some response. He also learnt from the poppy that in order to maintain this position the flower had to have a straight stem, and so he began to straighten up his spine.

He had read in some of the writings of the *Philokalia* that the monk ought to be slightly stooped, at times even painfully so, with eyes turned towards the heart and navel.

He asked Fr. Seraphim for a few clarifications. The eyes of the staretz looked at him with contempt. 'The holy men of old blazed with energy and this stooped posture was to call them back to the humility of their human condition. It did them no harm. But you need your energy. So, when meditating, be vigilant and hold yourself straight. And don't be proud. If you watch the poppy closely, it will teach you not only an upright posture but also how to bend with the wind. It will teach you humility.'

The poppy was also fragile. Its blossom soon faded. The young man understood that it was necessary not only to blossom but to wither. He understood the words of the prophet: 'All humanity is grass and all its beauty like the wild flowers. The grass withers and the flower fades ... The nations are like a drop in a bucket ... The rulers of the world are scarcely planted, scarcely sown, scarcely has their stem taken root in the soil, than they wither and the storm carries them away like chaff' (Is 40.6–7, 15, 24).

The mountain had given him a sense of eternity, the poppy was of time. To meditate is to know the Eternal in the fleetingness of the moment, to flower in the time we are given, to love in the time we are given for loving, without asking why. Why do poppies blossom?

Thus he learnt how to meditate 'without purpose or profit', but for the simple pleasure of being and of loving the light. 'Love itself is its own reward', said St Bernard. 'The rose blossoms because it blossoms, without why', said Angelus Silesius. 'It is the mountain that flowers in the poppy', thought the young man. 'The entire universe meditates in me. May it know joy for the brief time that my life lasts.' This thought was doubtless a bit too much. When he told it to Fr. Seraphim, the monk started shaking the young philosopher and once again took him by the arm and led him along a narrow path along the edge of the sea to an empty cave. 'Stop ruminating like a cow on the significance of the poppy. Think of the ocean. Learn to meditate like the ocean.'

To Meditate like the Ocean

The young man had acquired a good posture and a proper frame of mind. What was he lacking? The old monk led him to the ocean. What could the lapping of the waves possibly teach him? But the ebb and flow of the sea awoke in him the memory of long evenings he had spent on the shore of the Atlantic, harmonizing his own breath with the

great breathing rhythm of the waves. 'I inhale; I exhale ...
Then, I am inhaled and I am exhaled. I let myself be
carried by my breath as by the waves.'

And so he floated on his back, carried along by the
rhythm of the ocean's breath. At first he lost consciousness. But soon the drop of water that was the young man
learnt to keep its form and awareness. He was no longer
carried away by the deepened rhythm of his breathing.
The drop of water kept its identity. It this way the young
man learnt that to meditate was to breathe deeply, to let
the breath's ebb and flow just be.

He also learnt that though there might be waves on the
surface, the ocean bed remained calm. Thoughts come and
go. They foam around us. But deep down the ocean is still.
Each day this became more alive in him, and he remembered the words of a poet who had influenced him as a
boy: 'Existence is an endless sea full of waves. Most people
perceive nothing but the waves of the sea. See how from
the depths of the sea innumerable waves appear on the
surface, while the sea remains hidden in the waves.'
Today the sea seemed to him less hidden in the waves. The
unity of all things seemed more obvious, without destroying their individual identity.

At the foundation of his own breath was there not *ruah,
pneuma*, the great breath of God? 'The one who listens
attentively to his own breathing,' said the old monk, 'is
not far from God.'

To Meditate like a Bird

'Just because you have a good posture, can sit up straight
and breathe like the ocean does not mean you are praying
like the hesychasts.' Fr. Seraphim told him, 'Now you've
got to learn to meditate like a bird.' So the old monk led
him to a small cell near his hermitage where there were
two turtle-doves. At first the cooing of these little creatures charmed, but before long they began to exasperate
the young philosopher. They chose to bill and coo just as

he was falling asleep. He asked the old monk what all this meant. He could cope with a mountain, a poppy, an ocean (although one might wonder what was Christian in all of them), but love-sick birds was simply too much.

Fr. Seraphim explained that in the Old Testament the word for meditation sometimes designated the cry of an animal; for example the roar of a lion (Isaiah 31.4), the chirping of swallows, and the song of the dove (Isaiah 38.14), but also the growling of a bear.

'There are no bears on Mount Athos,' Fr. Seraphim continued, 'only turtle-doves. But the teaching is the same. You've got to meditate with your chest not simply to take in breath but also to recite the name of God day and night. To meditate is to coo like the turtle-dove, to let this song rise within you, just as you learnt to let the scent of the flower rise within you. To meditate is to breathe while singing. When you are happy, almost without being aware of it, you sometimes sing; you sometimes murmur words with no particular meaning, which make your entire body resound with a simple and serene joy. Without delaying too much over the meaning just now, I suggest you repeat, murmur, sing something that is in the heart of all the monks of Mount Athos: *"Kyrie eleison, Kyrie eleison ..."* (Lord have mercy).'

This didn't exactly thrill the young philosopher. He had heard this chant at weddings and funerals.

Fr. Seraphim started laughing: 'Well, yes, this is one of the meanings of the invocation, but there are many others as well. It can also mean "Lord, send forth your Spirit! Let your gentleness be upon me and upon everyone. May your name be blessed." But don't try too hard to grasp the meaning of this invocation. It will reveal itself to you. For now just be open and attentive to the way it sounds in your body and in your heart. Try to harmonize it with your breath. Whenever your thoughts torment you, return gently to this invocation. Breathe deeply. Sit up straight and perfectly still and you will know the beginning of still-ness, the peace that God gives freely.'

After a few days this '*Kyrie eleison*' became a little more familiar to the young philosopher. It accompanied him the way buzzing accompanies a bee when it makes honey. He didn't always repeat it with his lips. The hum gradually entered his heart.

This invocation, whose meaning he had stopped thinking about, sometimes led him into a silence he had never known before, and he compared himself to the Apostle Thomas when he had discovered the Risen Christ, '*Kyrie eleison*, my Lord and my God'. The invocation generated in him a deep respect for every living thing and an adoration of the One who remains hidden in the depths of things.

The old monk said to him, 'Now, you're not far from meditating like a human being.'

To Meditate like Abraham

Up to now the teaching of the staretz has been purely natural and therapeutic. The ancient monks, according to the testimony of Philo of Alexandria were 'therapists' of sorts. They sought to heal human nature, to put it in the best possible condition for receiving grace, a grace that does not destroy human nature but restores and completes it.

This healing is what the old monk has been doing with the young philosopher while teaching him a purely natural way of meditation, the mountain, the poppy, the ocean, the birds. Humanity has often lost contact with these natural elements which go together to form our macrocosm, and this often leads to all sorts of discomfort, sickness, insecurity and anxiety. The human being feels unwelcome, estranged from the world. That's why to meditate was first of all to enter into the meditation and praise of the entire universe. For, as the Fathers say, 'these things pray already'. In us the world's prayer becomes conscious and names what the rest of creation only mutters. With the meditation of Abraham, we enter into that new and higher awareness called Faith, an awareness of a Thou who manifests Himself in the intimate exchange of all things. It is in all things but it cannot be grasped by all things. The difference between Nature and God is the difference between the blue of the sky and the blue of one's eyes. Abraham was in search of these eyes.

The young man was thus invited to wakefulness of heart. 'Behold, suddenly you are someone.' The nature of the heart is to personalize everything and, in this case, to personalize the Absolute, the Source of all that lives and breathes, to name it, to call it 'my God and my Creator' and to walk in His presence. This form of meditation enters into every aspect of life.

The biblical story of the oak of Mamre shows us Abraham, seated in his tent, giving hospitality to three strangers who reveal that they are messengers of God. Fr. Seraphim said, 'to meditate like Abraham is to practise hospitality. Meditating like Abraham, you see, not only awakens in you peace and light, but also love for all people. The glass of water you give to the one who is thirsty does not disturb your silence; it brings you to its very source.' Fr. Seraphim read the famous passage from Genesis where Abraham stood before YHWH, who is, who was and who will be and says, 'Will you really destroy the upright with the guilty? Suppose there are fifty upright people in the city. Will you really destroy it? Will you not spare the place for the sake of the fifty upright in it?' (Gn 18.23–24).

Abraham gradually reduces the number of the upright needed to preserve Sodom. 'I trust my Lord will not be angry if I speak once more: perhaps there will only be ten ...' (Gn 18.32). To meditate like Abraham is to intercede for others, to know their suffering and never to despair of God's mercy.

This type of meditation frees the heart of its obsessive need to judge and condemn. Whatever the horrors that come one's way, pardon and blessings are invoked. To meditate like Abraham leads one still further.

At this point the old monk began to stumble over his

words. It was as if he wanted to spare the young man an experience which he himself had had to undergo. 'It can take you to the point of Sacrifice.' He cited a passage from Genesis where Abraham showed himself ready to sacrifice his own son, Isaac. 'It's all for God,' he muttered. 'Everything is from God, by God, and for God. To meditate like Abraham leads you to a loss of self and what you hold most dear. Look for what you hold onto the most, what you most identify with as your "I". For Abraham it was his only son. If you are capable of this total abandonment, of this unlimited trust in the One who transcends all reason and common sense, all will be given back to you a hundredfold. God will provide. To meditate like Abraham is to have in your heart and in your awareness nothing but God. When he arrives at the top of the mountain, Abraham thinks of nothing but his son. When he returns back down, he thinks of nothing but God.

To pass over the mountain of Sacrifice is to discover that nothing belongs to this "I". Everything belongs to God. To meditate like Abraham is to cling by faith to the One who transcends the world of things. It is to practise hospitality and to intercede for the salvation of all. It is to forget yourself in order to discover that you, your neighbour and the entire Universe are the dwelling place of the infinite presence of the God who Is.'

To Meditate like Jesus

Fr. Seraphim became more and more discreet. He sensed the progress that the young man was making in meditation and prayer: a face bathed with tears often surprised the old monk as the young man meditated like Abraham, interceding for humanity. 'My God, my Mercy, what will become of those who have lost the way?'

One day the young man approached Fr. Seraphim and asked: 'Father, why don't you ever speak to me of Jesus? What was his own prayer like, his way of meditation? In the liturgy and in the sermons, one hears only of him. In the prayer of the heart, such as we read of in *The Philokalia*, one calls upon the name of Jesus. Why don't you ever say anything about this?'

The old monk looked troubled, as if the young man had asked him to reveal his deepest secrets. The greater the revelation, the greater the humility required to pass it on. Doubtless the old monk did not consider himself humble enough. 'Only the Holy Spirit can teach you that. "No one knows who the Son is except the Father, and who the Father is except the Son and those to whom the Son chooses to reveal him" (Lk 10.22). You have to become a child of God in order to pray like the Son and have His relationship with the one who sent him, his Father, and *that* is the work of the Holy Spirit. The Holy Spirit will remind you of everything Jesus said. The Gospel will become something alive in you and will teach you to pray as you should.'

The young man insisted, 'Tell me more.'

The old monk smiled. 'It's probably better simply to tell you outright. To meditate like Jesus perfects all the forms of meditation that I have passed on to you. Jesus is the cosmic person. He knows how to meditate like a mountain, like a poppy, like an ocean, like the turtle-dove. He knows how to meditate like Abraham. His is the boundless heart that loves even its enemies, its executioners: "Father forgive them, for they know not what they do." He offers hospitality to the sick, the sinner, the paralytic, the prostitute, the tax collector. At night he steals away to pray in secret and cries out like a child, "Abba", which means "daddy". It may sound ridiculous to call God "Daddy" but that was Jesus' prayer, and in it Heaven and earth were united. God and humankind become one. One day this "Abba" will arise not from your lips but from the depths of your heart. On that day you will begin to understand exactly what the prayer and meditation of the hesychasts is.'

Now Go!

The young man remained on Mount Athos another few months. The Jesus Prayer swept him into the abyss. At times he was on the verge of madness. He could say with St Paul, it is no longer I whom you see but Christ living in me. It was the folly of humility, of intercession, of desire that all be saved. He became love. He became fire. Like the Burning Bush he was burned but not consumed. A remarkable luminous quality visited his body.

That was when Fr. Seraphim began to growl. 'That's enough! Now go!' He asked him to leave Mount Athos and return home. There he would see what remained of his silent prayer!

So the young man left and returned home. He had lost weight, and nobody found his filthy beard and neglected appearance spiritual at all. But life in the city did not make him forget the teaching of the old monk.

When he was feeling agitated or pressed for time, he would sit like a mountain. Whenever he felt pride or conceit, he would remember the poppy, that 'every flower withers'. When sadness, anger or disgust overtook him, he would breathe deeply like the ocean and rediscover his own breath in the breath of God, invoking God's Name and crying softly, '*Kyrie eleison*'. If he saw human suffering, misfortune or weakness, he remembered the meditation of Abraham. If anyone slandered him, he was happy to pray with Christ. He didn't try to be a saint. He even forgot his silent prayer. He simply tried to love God from moment to moment and to walk in his Presence.

Chapter Two

Arsenius, or the Beginning of Hesychasm

Arsenius is well known amongst hesychasts. In the Egyptian deserts of former times, as in Orthodox monasteries of our own day, his story has been often told. The Greek word *soteria* means to have a big heart, to breathe deeply, to be free, to be in full health. It was this word which was used to mean 'salvation' in the New Testament, and one day Arsenius prayed to God, asking how might one achieve *soteria*. He did not ask what was the meaning of life or why was there evil; he asked for something to do, to live, to experience.

The Lord answered with three brief words: flee, be silent, repose. Each of these words, like the words of Scripture, can be understood on different levels. First of all in a literal sense, then in a psychological and finally in a spiritual sense. Each of these words asks us to perform a *mitzvah*, an exercise or precept to recover the health of spirit, soul and body and become once again the image and likeness of God.

Flee

Arsenius, like all the desert fathers, took this word literally. One must take flight, leave, depart, flee the world and its worldliness. Flee because it is suffocating. To flee is not lack of nerve but surfeit of health. To flee is the great strength of the hind. When one perceives that the environment has become menacing, capable of smothering or perverting what good one has, it is better to go elsewhere. In its first sense to take flight is to change locale, environment, lifestyle. For adolescents to flee or to run away is a survival reflex, a vital necessity; there is no pleasure to be found in dead-end situations. The ancient monks left the world because they saw no other way out but death. A strange desire made them think that they were not born simply to die, but that another Space, 'whether in the body or out of the body' (2 Co 12.3) awaited them. The physical desert is located at the frontiers of space and time. There is nothing to see, nothing to find. It's a good place for light.

This fleeing can, nevertheless, be taken in a negative sense: to flee *from* something rather than take flight *for* something. Ascetic texts are rather clear on this: one must flee evil and all that excites it and makes it grow. In other words, flee what leads to sin.

For the ancient monks sin meant 'to miss the mark' (the literal sense of the New Testament word *hamartia*). Various texts from the *Philokalia* develop this sense along the lines of forgetfulness of Being. Mark the Hermit says, 'Whenever you remember God, increase your prayer so that when the day comes when you forget Him, the Lord might make you remember.'

Scripture says, 'Sheol and Perdition lie open to Yahweh' (Pr 15.11). Sheol means ignorance, perdition, forgetfulness of heart. It is necessary to flee the world because in the world is much forgetfulness.

In the desert it is impossible to forget who and what we are. Our fragility brings us back to the Living One, 'in whom we live and move and have our being'. We discover once again our essential axis. We re-learn how to hit the mark. This is what it means to leave sin behind. The memory of the Living One quickens life within us. It centres us on the contemplation of the One who is at the heart of who we are. Nonetheless we remain ever free to turn from Being, to distract ourselves from it. In this sense it is rather the world which is fleeing from the essential; it is cowardice before the fact of our nothingness.

If the desert fathers have often mentioned flight from the world as the point of departure for salvation, they have insisted still more on this flight as a fleeing *towards* someone. And the philosopher Plotinus spoke of the flight 'of the alone to the Alone'. Their flight was a procession of clarity and knowledge but it was even more their heart's own impulse, their desire to know as they were known (1 Corinthians 13.12), to love as they were loved.

Artists, musicians, writers often need to flee even their closest relationships in order to free themselves up entirely for their creative work. Their solitude is not a rejection of society but a contribution to it. As Henri Laborit, one of the great contemporary biologists, makes clear in his book, *In Praise of Flight*: solitude is necessary for creativity.

One can flee into drugs, work, the imagination, obedience or fatalism. What is important is to know from what we are fleeing. Did Arsenius know what he was fleeing from? Without doubt he fled from the illusion of what he thought himself to be. Above all he fled towards Someone. This is the spiritual meaning of flight. It is the affirmation of transcendence, that there is something in this world that is not of this world, that the world does not contain within itself its own meaning. This perspective has sometimes caused Christians to be viewed rather suspiciously by political regimes which see nothing beyond the world and nothing that does not refer to their own power.

To renounce the world is to affirm one's own liberty. The origin of the Hebrew word for sanctity suggests the idea of separation. The saint is one who stands apart, who lives in another way. Israel is considered a holy people because it is separated from the world and given to God. For the desert fathers also, sanctity is to keep a certain distance from the world and its ways.

The great model of all those who 'take flight' is Abraham, who left family and homeland in search of God and the land that God would show him (Genesis 12.1). From a psychological point of view it is necessary to leave father and mother in order to assume one's own autonomy.

It is well to remember that Jesus was one of those who fled. As a child of twelve he used to slip away from his parents and visit the Temple. 'Do you not know that I must be about my Father's business?' Jesus wants to know God. From God alone comes life and the meaning of life.

Arsenius, like Abraham, fled from established certainties to follow the uncertainty of his desire through the darkness of night. Our deepest desire is oriented towards grace. We seek what cannot be possessed. We desire Someone who cannot be possessed. God does not fulfil desire. He empties it out and makes the so-called objects of desire seem unreal by substituting Himself who cannot be possessed. Son of Abraham that he was, Arsenius advanced into the night as though he saw the Invisible.

But what gain is there in fleeing the world? The world is within us. Does not the body hold in each and every muscle, nerve and cell the memory of its *miasmata*? Anthony of the Desert made the hallucinations of the desert monks famous; there are few streets in the world as rich in temptation as the imagination of a hermit.

Cassian tells the story of a man who entered a monastery and handed over all his possessions. But after many years in his cell he considered a simple eraser too precious and could not bring himself to loan it to any of his brethren. This example proves that it matters little whether a bird is attached by a thread or by a chain. It is unable to fly just the same.

In the desert, attachment is even more subtle. While you might not be attached to material goods, you could well be attached to ideas or religious observances. As long as you have not forgotten yourself everything is an excuse for attachment. That is why the hesychastic tradition insists on obedience to a spiritual father as a sure means of deliverance. When you remove from Narcissus his will-fulness and satisfaction with his own image, he finds himself in the desert of God. Otherwise even when he prays he is regarding himself in the mirror.

Like Arsenius each of us knows what must be left behind in order to live in freedom. The most visible chains are not always the most gripping. What is this invisible thread which even in destitution makes us still say 'me'? Some people immersed in the heart of the world live in a more detached way, ready to breathe their last at the Source of all Breath. Others, who have officially renounced the world, jealously guard their own emotional security.

Even more than Abraham, Arsenius's model was Christ himself. The Gospel often shows Him fleeing the crowd, not only when it wanted to crown him king, but also at night when he would flee towards the One whom he called his Father: 'The world must know that I love my Father.' He even maintained this distance with his disciples in order to show them where his treasure was, where his heart was. On the day of the Ascension, he departed once and for all. 'It is good for you that I go.' He left in order to prepare a place. 'If I do not go, the Spirit of Truth will not be able to come. When He does come He will remind you of everything I told you ... that you are in me and I in you.'

Christ effaces Himself so as not to become an idol, someone sought from the outside. Rather Christ wants to be our own inner life. We must flee from physical representations of Christ in order to rediscover the Source. As Meister Eckhart says: 'It is for love of God that we take leave of God.'

It sometimes happens that in our own spiritual life we feel that God or Christ flees from us. Christ withdraws. But He remains the same yesterday, today and always. Only the false images we have of Him depart along with our relent-less need for gratifying objects. Our beliefs disintegrate and faith emerges, the pure clinging to the emptiness of our needs and to the Unknown who leads us.

Be Silent

The second word Arsenius hears is 'be silent'. Ghandi, who spent one day a week in silence, reminds us that silence is a pre-condition for health. We use energy in speaking and by silence we restore this energy. Thus we become capable of words worthy of silence, words as powerful as the Word.

Therefore, the practice of silence is to be taken first of all in the literal sense. St James says that someone who can control his tongue, can control his whole body (see James 3.2). Pythagorus said, 'More difficult than all other arts is the art of mastering one's own tongue.'

With just the right word one can heal, console or teach, but one can also murder, maim or lie. We will be held accountable for every word, says the Evangelist. What more could make us want to be silent? Every ill-founded word judges us, reveals our pretentious ignorance. Scientists are well aware that reality is ever escaping them, that what was once considered a well-founded certitude according to generations of scientists does not withstand the scrutiny of ever more perfect instruments. Just as these instruments shake the foundation of certain quantum realities, so the desert fathers were aware of the ravages of calumny and slander.

There is the story of the young monk who had a sharp tongue ever ready to comment on the pious behaviour of his confrères. An older monk said to him: 'Go and find me a turkey.' The young monk produced it. 'Now pluck its feathers.' He obeyed. Once the turkey was plucked the old monk said: 'Now put its feathers back on.' The young man, somewhat shocked, asked: 'How am I supposed to do that? You can't put feathers back on a plucked turkey.'

'Right you are,' said the old man kindly. 'Just as you can't repair the reputation of someone whom you have destroyed with your tongue. Take care not to slander your neighbour.' As the proverb says, 'You can always find something to gossip about.' Only the holy ones know how to keep the heart calm in the face of calumny. Recent history shows us the example of people who have not survived the loss of their reputations. Sometimes what led them to internment or suicide was a mere rumour, an ill-founded word.

Other Gospel writings invite one to silence. 'Make a tree sound and its fruit will be sound; make a tree rotten and its fruit will be rotten. For the tree can be told by its fruit. You brood of vipers, how can your speech be good when you are evil? For words flow out of what fills the heart. Good people draw good things from their store of good-ness; bad people draw bad things from their store of badness. So I tell you this, that for every unfounded word people utter they will answer on Judgement Day, since it is by your words you will be justified, and by your words condemned' (Mt 12.33–37).

'What goes into the mouth does not make anyone unclean; it is what comes out of the mouth that makes someone unclean' (Mt 15.11).

St Isaac the Syrian insists that when a person sees every-one as good and no one as impure, then one can say that that person has truly attained purity of heart. Everything is pure for one who is pure.

The ancient monks used to remind novices that in order to arrive at this interior silence, the non-judgement of humble love, they must first learn to restrain from speak-ing behind someone's back.

To become silent brings us ultimately to the abyss of Silence. Ignatius of Antioch speaks of the silence of the Father, the Source of the Word which proceeds from the Father and returns home to the Father. To become silent enables us to listen. Prayer is not just talking to God but listening to – sometimes enduring – the silence of God. 'Hear, O Israel' is the first commandment.

To become silent is to become receptive to God, like Mary who 'listened and pondered all these things in her heart'. The word of Jesus to Arsenius, which at first sight might seem negative, conceals something quite positive.

To pray, flee all noise, interior and exterior, and in silence listen to Him who Is. The fathers of the desert used to say that silence is not something you create. It is already there, like a white page that remains immaculate between the lines. It is enough to remove the words, to stop talking. Happy are they who understand the words of Jesus, but happier still are they who listen to His silence.

In the desert, exterior silence is the servant of inner silence. It is enough to become quiet to set off all the internal discourse and commentary on all our actions. Good therapists that they were, each evening the old monks used to ask their novices to put into words the thoughts which had tormented them during the day. They called this 'expelling the venom from the mouth of the serpent'. The venom was different for each person. What can torment someone alone in the silence of the desert more than the heavy burden of memories – every unsatisfied desire, every hatred unexpressed, resentments and regrets that won't loosen their grip? The old monks knew better than to exacerbate this obsession with guilt. They said, 'If your heart condemns you, God is greater than your heart.' To recognize your sin does not add to it. It is not to pour salt on the wound or to return to your vomit. It is simply to acknowledge the difficulty of staying in the divine presence and asking deliverance from those memories which prevent the contemplation of God.

If the interior discourse became too noisy or threatening, the old monks would suggest doing as the Psalm bids: 'dash the heads of the children of Babylon against the rock'. The children of Babylon are our thoughts. The rock is the name of Jesus. What is at the origin of fear, anguish, and selfish desire? A thought. And at this thought we must take aim from the very start, substituting for it that human-divine Name of invincible love, Jesus.

Solitude, silence and the invocation of the Name comprise (from the earliest centuries) the fundamental elements of the practice of silence. The goal is to attain 'inviolable tranquillity of the heart', as Cassian puts it. It is to attain that silence of the heart that does not judge or scheme or plot. Only the silent heart can love truly not only God in contemplation but also others as they are, not as we would have them. Silence makes us present to what *is*, without insisting that they somehow measure up to some expectation. To love as God loves, that is, as God creates a person at that precise moment.

But who can remain silent in the face of crime and injustice? Doesn't the Bible condemn the 'silent dogs' who watch without saying a word against innocent suffering? Does not Scripture say, 'Wisdom concealed, and treasure undiscovered, what use is either of these? Better one who conceals his folly than one who conceals his widsom' (Si 20.30–31).

We must not make an idol of silence. Like our words, the value of silence is the weight of love which dwells in it and leavens it. How many heavy silences compared with this loving silence?

For the old monks silence of the lips should lead to silence of the heart, which itself can lead to silence of the spirit. But this last silence is a gift which one cannot acquire by effort, asceticism or hope. It is a desire which has not entered the human heart. At this moment, when time and eternity embrace, one no longer even thinks of God. God is there. The words of prayer vanish before His Presence. As a monk of Mount Athos once said: 'When you are with someone, you don't think about him or her, they are right there. True prayer is not thinking about God. It is being with God. Letting God be. To let God breathe in our breath.'

Isaac the Syrian recalls that language was created in time. Silence belongs to eternity. A word always has something of the ego. True silence is beyond ego.

'Be silent'. Do not think 'preserve the silence'. Think rather 'silence preserves me'. In the middle of the fray, at the eye of the storm, constant as a magnet, silence calls me to rest.

Repose

The last word which Arsenius received was 'repose' or 'be at rest'. The monks of the West, especially the Carthusians, speak of this rest (*quies*) as the goal of Christian life. It is what the Greek monks called *hesychia* and the Hebrews called *shalom*, the peace of God.

'Find interior peace,' said St Seraphim, 'and an entire multitude will be saved along with you.' It is as though the salvation of all depends on our inner peace. If one believes what physicists tell us about the interconnectedness of all things, that it is impossible to remove one sprig of straw without disturbing a star, it is not so difficult to believe that a person of deep peace communicates some of this calm and serenity to the whole world. One never meditates for oneself alone. Moreover, the Book of Widsom says that God seeks amongst people a place of rest. A peaceful person is a dwelling place of God. Hence it is easy to understand the importance which *hesychia* enjoyed amongst the early monks. Without it God could not dwell amongst humans. After agitation has been left behind, silence of the lips and heart have no other purpose than to lead to this repose.

This is the meaning of Sabbath, the repose of the seventh day. Humanity has received a mission other than doing, producing, accumulating goods, information and power. Humanity has received the mission of being ever more intimate with the One who is being itself, to the point of union. We work in order to rest. Our labours in the desert make no sense if they are not energized by this sacred meaning of hesychasm.

Respect for the Sabbath is a commandment. Irrespective of social class, of the masks we wear or of our role in society, we discover in the Sabbath our identity as children of God. The least known and most important human right is the right to contemplation. But contemplation is never as easy as it looks. It is the fruit and sign of a personality in harmony with itself and with God.

By dint of looking for peace many have lost it! Their hearts of flesh have become hearts of stone. Some finish their lives as mad megalomaniacs or depressives, if they have not become cruel or desperate.

Peace of heart is the desire of all but the experience of a few.

Repose. Be at rest. Perhaps we should take this command first of all in the physical sense of relax. A certain tension, whether muscular or nervous, can prevent us not only from feeling well but also from being receptive to another dimension. A contemporary Orthodox monk has said, 'You do not pray the same with your bum tensed as when it is relaxed.' A tense person is less open to God's presence. To relax is to open wider one's doors whether these be sensory (the doors of perception), affective, or intellectual.

If you just recall a wonderful moment of relaxation in a meadow, you may have wondered where the earth began and where your body ended. The calm of the desert was not sought out for the well-being it brought, but as a means of receptivity towards another, the complete Other. Without doubt it would be better to say 'let go', to loosen the grip of ego, the will to succeed at any price. This would be one's meditation or prayer. But everyone has heard the story of the man who pushed and pushed to open the door. When he finally quit, utterly exhausted, the door opened ... from the other side. We think we seek God, but it is God who seeks us. Our task is not to take God but to receive God. The tragedy of Prometheus is that he wanted to steal the fire which God wanted to give. In his efforts to seize he lost his ability to receive. Freedom and inner peace are not acquisitions but gifts received, gifts which disappear the moment you try to possess them. Amongst the desert monks there were not a few like Prometheus who began their assault on God as though he were a very high mountain. They never knew repose.

The great enemy of repose is worry. Jesus asked his disciples not to worry themselves and gave them as examples the model of the birds and lilies. 'That is why I am telling you not to worry about your life and what you are to eat, nor about your body and what you are to wear. Surely life is more than food, and the body more than clothing! Look at the birds in the sky. They do not sow or reap or gather into barns; yet your heavenly Father feeds them. Are you not worth much more than they are? Can any of you, however much you worry, add one single cubit to your span of life? And why worry about clothing? Think of the flowers growing in the fields; they never have to work or spin; yet I assure you that not even Solomon in all his royal robes was clothed like one of these. Now if that is how God clothes the wild flowers growing in the field which are there today and thrown into the furnace tomorrow, will he not much more look after you, you who have so little faith? So do not worry; do not say, "What are we to eat? What are we to drink? What are we to wear?" It is the gentiles who set their hearts on all these things. Your heavenly Father knows you need them all. Set your hearts on his kingdom first, and on God's saving justice, and all these other things will be given you as well. So do not worry about tomorrow: tomorrow will take care of itself. Each day has enough trouble of its own' (Mt 6.25–34).

Many idle, heedless and irresponsible people will be able to avail themselves of the words of Jesus to justify their more or less aberrant behaviour. There remains nonetheless according to the most severe of the desert ascetics *amerimnia*, or the fact of being without worry. It is one of the most important conditions for achieving hesychia. To this John Climacus devoted his twenty-seventh step in *The Ladder of Divine Ascent*. He writes, 'The principle work of hesychia is a perfect *amerimnia* with regard to all things rational and irrational.' If we could only free ourselves of those things which only get in the way, either because they are bad in themselves or are of absolutely no use in the spiritual life, nothing would make more sense. But why would it be necessary to act the same towards those things which seem justified with good reason?

Climacus gives two psychological reasons. First, one worry leads to another. 'The one who opens the door to sound reasons will clutter the mind just as surely as with unsound reasons.' Finally, interior stillness is a state of mind which allows no compromise. It is all or nothing. 'The smallest hair irritates the eye, and the slightest worry makes stillness vanish.' But this stillness is not an end in itself. If the mind is freed entirely of all that could agitate it, however small, it is with a view to disposing oneself to contemplation. 'The one who would bring before God a pure mind and yet lets oneself be troubled by worry is like the person who shackles one's own feet and then pretends to hate walking.'

More than likely John Climacus has in a mind a line from Evagrius. 'A person bound in chains cannot run, nor can the mind when subjected to passion see the place of spiritual prayer. For the soul is pulled along here and there by the effects of passionate thoughts and cannot hold itself firm.'[1]

But one must go further still. For Climacus, stillness is not merely the elimination of legitimate worry; it is also the elimination of concepts in the widest sense of the term. 'You will not attain pure prayer if you are obstructed by material goods or bothered by continuous worry, for prayer is the elimination of concepts.'[2]

The absence of thought is self-forgetfulness. When the mind is calm, the 'little I' gradually disappears. It opens up to the Otherness which is its ground and there finds rest.

The calming of the mind is also the calming of desire. The monastic learns to be content with what he or she has: 'Desire all that you have and you will have all you desire.' This contentment was thought to be a virtue capable of liberating the monastic from the temptation to compare himself or herself with others. In monastic environs the

---

[1] Evagrius, *On Prayer*, ch. 71.
[2] Evagrius, *On Prayer*, ch. 70.

demon of comparison could be quite fierce. Where there is jealousy there is no peace.

The great secret of interior peace is humility. It is well known that one of the sources of anguish and anxiety is to test the difference between who one pretends to be and who one really is. To be as you are, adding nothing, taking nothing away, pretending no longer, accepting your earthiness, strengths and weaknesses. Angels are vastly more humble than humans because they are much more intelligent. To be intelligent is to know yourself. If you know yourself, you know you are nothing. What could bother someone who considered himself nothing, not in a psychological sense – that would be self-deprecating and pathological – but in an ontological sense, to know that your being is not of your own creation? This brings us to another synonym for repose to which Christ invites Arsenius: trust.

The believer knows freedom. The believer does not worry because she knows her life does not depend on her. This is not apathy of fatalism but clear-sighted faith in God who leads us through unknown paths.

To be humble is simply to be human. To be human means not taking ourselves for God, and this makes us capable of receiving God, to live with God. We enter another dimension, no longer in the world and threatened by the law of entropy, whatever might be our attempts to maintain a life whose nature it is to pass away.

'I leave you peace, my peace I give you, not as the world gives.' The world gives us tranquillizers and antidepressants, but the peace at issue here is an ontological or deeper peace. It depends on nothing and on no one. It cannot be limited to the psychological level or to techniques which induce tranquillity (like drugs these techniques can lead to dependency). It roots itself at the spiritual. It is the peace of God, God's breath, God's presence in us.

Our peace is Another. In this sense one can say that it does not depend on us and that it can abide even when the psychological 'I' suffers the worst torments. This Other, which no one can take from us does not dwell in space and time.

'I am overflowing with joy in the midst of my sufferings,' claimed St Paul. Inconceivable joy for the one who has awakened to this Presence, who is at once more me than myself and more other than myself.

One could say of Arsenius, who came to know this repose, that 'he is separated from all yet united to all, imperturbable yet utterly sensitive, deified yet acutely human. More than anyone else he is happy, divinely happy' (Evagrius).

Flee! Be silent! Repose! These three words received by Arsenius are often cited by the desert fathers.

The word 'hesychast' is often translated as 'solitary', 'silent' or 'person of peace'. Arsenius can be considered the archetypal person in search of God who takes literally the words which come to his heart.

He points to a path, a practice of simplification and opening to the one who came so that we might 'have life and have it to the full', a life not of anguish and torment but of peace and abundance. This is not a view of life as preparation for death but of life as preparation for Resurrection and Eternal Rest.

Chapter Three

The Purification of Thoughts according to Evagrius Ponticus

We know of Evagrius through the chapter which his disciple, Palladius, dedicates to him in *The Lausiac History*. He was born in 345 at Ibora in Pontus, not far from the family estate of Basil the Great in Annisa, where the latter, together with Gregory of Nazianzus, would spend 357–358 in a sort of monastic experiment. Hence, from early on Evagrius had ties with the great Cappadocians, and it was Gregory of Nazianzus who ordained him deacon. As a young man he made a name for himself by his sharp mind and gift for argument in the various controversies of the day.

A failed love forced him to flee Constantinople (where Gregory of Nazianzus had brought him) to Jerusalem. There he was received by Melania the Elder and Rufinus, who ultimately convinced him to pursue the monastic life in Egypt. There, in the cells of Nitrius and Scete, he was initiated into the wisdom of the desert, a wisdom that the learned of this world did not know, the wisdom of transformation, of conversion (*metanoia*). It is above all a practice which presumes profound self-knowledge – conscious and unconscious.

Besides Basil and Gregory, his teachers were Macarius, Amnanias, the great reader of Origen, and Abba Pambo.

Patriarch Theophilus wanted to make Evagrius a bishop, but, being a good monk, he refused. According to Palladius, Evagrius died in 399, aged fifty-four.

His writings are abundant. He describes the basics of monastic life and the life of prayer, but he is known above all for the *Praktikos* and the *Gnostikos*, wherein he shows, in the spirit of the Gospel, but also under the influence of Origen, the goal of the Christian life and the means for arriving at this goal.

We are going to study the *Praktikos*, the famous treatise that will later be transmitted to the West almost literally by John Cassian. This enjoyed a tremendous success in Western monasticism up to the Counter Reformation.

What is 'praktikos' or ascetic practice? 'The ascetic life is that spiritual method which purifies the passionate part of the soul' (Chapter 78). It is the slow work of purifying the heart – conscious and unconscious – in order to redicover one's original beauty, health or salvation (*soteria* in Greek).

You might say that Evagrius's *Praktikos* is a fourth-century treatise on therapy, the goal of which is to guide one to the knowledge of one's true nature as the image and likeness of God, free of all its pathologies. In this sense one could translate the Greek world *apatheia*, used by both Evagrius and the entire desert tradition, not as 'impassibility' but as 'non-pathological state' of the human, if, that is, it is true that conversation 'consists', as St John Damascene says, 'in moving from what is contrary to nature towards what is proper to it'. Ascetic practice in this sense is a form of psychoanalysis. It is an analysis of the movements of body and soul, impulses and passions, its thoughts which ambush the soul and which cause aberrant behaviour. Hence the essential element in this desert practice will consist of the analysis of and fight against what Evagrius calls *'logismoi'*, which we will translate literally as 'thoughts'.

Later on, the Christian tradition will refer to these thoughts as demons or *diaboloi* in Greek (literally that which divides the human against itself, that which fragments). The word in Hebrew is connected to *shatan*, the obstacle (that which sets itself in opposition to unity within, with others and with God). It is a question of discerning what blocks the realization of one's deepest self, what impedes the fulfilment of the life of the Spirit (*pneuma*) in one's being, thought and action.

Evagrius identifies eight thoughts at the root of our behaviour, which are symptoms of a spiritual sickness, thoughts that pollute a person, put him in a state of sin (*hamartia*):

1. *Gastrimargia* (Cassian will translate directly from the Greek, *de spiritu gastrimargiae*). Gluttony and all forms of oral pathology.
2. *Philarguria* (Cassian: *de spiritu philarguriae*). Avarice and all forms of retentiveness and constipation.
3. *Porneia* (Cassian: *de spiritu fornicatione*). Impurity: fornication, masturbation and every manner of sexual obsession, but also every manner of sexual obsession, deviation or genital compensation.
4. *Orgé* (Cassian: *de spiritu irae*). Anger. A disease of the irascible appetite.
5. *Lupé* (Cassian: *de spiritu tristitiae*). Depression, sadness, melancholy.
6. *Akedia* (Cassian: *de spiritu acediae*). Listlessness, suicidal depression, despair, the death instinct.
7. *Kenodoxia* (Cassian: *de spiritu cenodoxiae*). Vainglory, ego-inflation.
8. *Hyperphania* (Cassian: *de spiritu superbiae*). Pride, paranoia, schizophrenic delirium.

These eight thoughts will have a long history – from John Cassian to Gregory the Great, who in his *Moralia* throws out *akedia* but introduces envy and combines *kenodoxia* and *hyperphania* (calling pride the queen of vices, thus reducing the number to seven. So these eight symptoms become known as the 'seven deadly sins' – a notion which is spread far and wide by the time of the Counter Reformation. Their medical character is gradually forgotten. But originally it was very much a question of analysing a type of psycho-spiritual cancer, a cancer of the will which gnawed away at body and soul, destroying their integrity. It is a question of analysing the pernicious influences which act upon freedom, causing a person to lose his or her sense of divine-human destiny. Let us look more closely at these patholgies and search for their cause and possible remedy.

Gluttony (Gastrimargia)

Certain childhood traumas, especially those involving the mother, can mark a child, particularly during the time of breastfeeding or weaning. Some adult behaviours show a fixation at this so-called 'oral phase' of development. Anxiety and distress can cause a person to regress into infantile coping strategies, seeking comfort in consuming food or drink (bulimia) or their absence (anorexia).

The ancient monks advised measure, balance and discretion to overcome the unconscious drives that fuelled these strategies. They prescribed moderate fasting and oral prayer – the chanting of hymns and psalms. In *The Way of a Pilgrim*, the pilgrim counsels a drunkard to read out loud the Gospel whenever he felt drawn to the bottle. This succeeded in calming him and removing his desire to drink.

Some have interpreted original sin as a sin of gluttony: the fruit, symbolizing the world, is taken as a consumer-product instead of the very centre of communion with Being, its Source and Creator.

To be freed from gluttony, from this spirit of consumption, a person must become able to live *eucharistically*. As St Paul said, 'Whatever you eat and drink, do it all for the glory of God.'

Avarice (Philarguria)

Avarice includes clinging to any sort of possession whatever it may be. Cassian tells the story of a monk who,
having left behind all his possessions when he entered the
monastery, was incapable of parting with an eraser. It was
stronger than he was. He could not loan it to his confrères.
The example illustrates the senseless attachments people
can have not only to material goods (an eraser, a book,
clothing) but also to ideas, customs, or to postures.

The roots of this behaviour belong to the so-called anal
stage. Little children are completely identified with their
bodies and are traumatized when they see the body
'decomposing' as faecal matter. If the mother is not there
to reassure and thank the child for this lovely gift, the
child might become frightened, leading to closing up the
sphincter or, the opposite, playing in the excrement. Potty
training is never simple, and everyone has, in the unconscious, more or less painful traces of this period which will
manifest themselves under the guise of bodily obsessions
(positive or negative), tensions or constipation. On a
psychological level it is a pathological clinging to accumulated goods.

The fathers of the desert seem to have perceived the
unconscious root of all this when they counselled their
monks to meditate on death and take stock of the fact that
everything will one day pass away and to free themselves
of their earthly possessions.

To be avaricious, to accumulate riches and keep them
for yourself alone is to maintain steam on the glass of our
existence but it will not prevent the steam from evaporat-
ing. For the desert fathers were very much concerned to
discover what in life was of lasting value. They advised
meditation on the passing nature of all things but also
meditation on that which does not pass away, the Uncreated, who dwells within us. The Gospel is not lacking in
parables concerning this theme: To leave the shadow for
the prize; to sell all one's possessions for the pearl of great

price; where your treasure is there also is your heart.

This treasure is transpersonal. It is divine life in each of us. It is love, that paradoxical treasure which increases in the measure that we consume it.

Thus for the ancient monks avarice was a serious illness in that it impaired the health of the heart, that is, generosity, communication and the sharing of life. Avarice cultivates fear of love. It deprives us of the pleasure of participating in the generosity and graciousness of God – for it is a greater pleasure to give than to receive.

Impurity (Porneia)

Porneia, or impurity, has to to with a poor psycho-physical equilibrium that polarizes all our energy at the genital level. It can involve any number of impulses which overwhelm the person and can create tensions which can only find an outlet in masturbation or sexual promiscuity.

At a deeper level the spirit of impurity causes a person to treat bodies as things without souls, objects of pleasure as opposed to subjects of love, made in the image and likeness of God.

For the ancient monks, chastity is more than physical continence. It includes an attitude of respect for oneself and for others, not viewing them as though they were objects. To touch them with your hands or dissect them with your mind is the same. Chastity restores the sense of mystery to a person, his or her 'non-consumable' otherness. People are not consumer products; they cannot be reduced to our needs and desires.

Evagrius offers practical advice to those who suffer from these painfully obsessive sexual urges – drink less fluid. For according to ancient medical thought, sexual arousal comes from the bodily system being too wet.[1]

Evagrius also recommends manual labour and meditation on the Scriptures. Since the brain is our principle

---

[1] See Hippocrates, *de generatione*, ed. Littré, vol. VII, Paris, 1851, p. 470.

sexual organ, it is a question of substituting an obsessive sexual thought with one of praise. In these difficult moments, it is not a question of leaving the mind empty, but of occupying it through the invocation of the Name, through chant or some other type of prayer. Moreover, one does not arrive at true chastity while being afraid to love, but, on the contrary, by loving all the more.

Anger (Orgé)

Orgé. The word is usually translated as 'anger' or 'impatience'. In Hebrew it is *qesôr ' appaim*, which literally means shortness of breath. Anger causes us to lose our breath. We have shallow breath. We suffocate as if possessed.

Evagrius attaches great importance to this phenomenon of anger. For him anger disfigures a person and renders him a demon. 'No vice makes the intellect become like a demon as much as anger; all due to some disturbance in the irascible part of the soul. The Psalm says "their anger is like a serpent" (Ps 57, 5). Don't think the demon is anything other than a person disturbed by anger' (Letter 56).

Anger, moreover, wreaks havoc upon the liver and excites the production of bile. Anger is especially dangerous when held within, unexpressed. It can lead to ulcers. It will produce nightmares and other disturbances of sleep.

One of the causes of anger comes from the difficulty in accepting others as they are. If they do not correspond to the image we have of them, we become angry and are eaten alive by our own resentment. It is a sign of immaturity (think of the anger of infants who want everything instantly), but there can also be the justified anger of the adult (but without hatred) such as indignation before an injustice, at righting the wrong and leading people back to the path of justice.

But what are the remedies for the unjust anger that alienates? First, pardon. To forgive others for not being the way we are. Next, learning to prolong the breath. This might seem sheer common sense, but it is also a spiritual exercise. In the language of the Bible, to express the idea that God is patient one says 'God has big nostrils' – a physical image that expresses God's calm and patience.

'Never let the sun set on your anger' (Ep 4.26). Maybe, before retiring, before being able to pardon their enemies, the old monks used to take a few deep breaths, gently prolonging the exhalation to chase off thoughts of anger, even perhaps enlarging their nostrils to acquire a divine patience. For Evagrius the great quality of the monk is gentleness, which is the very opposite of anger. It is what distinguishes Moses and Jesus from all the others. This gentleness was not softness or weakness but the Holy Spirit's mastery of the irascible appetite, a reflection of the harmonization, by the Spirit, of all physical and psychic faculties.

Sadness (Lupé)

Every type of frustration involves in some way a state of sadness (*lupé*). But the Christian life is joy and peace in the Holy Spirit. To attain this one must fight against sadness and face frustration and deprivation.

To be an adult, according to the desert fathers, is to take on willingly the deprivation, but the ascetism of will is more in its orientation than in its non-satisfaction. To endure willingly a certain number of frustrations on the material level but especially on the emotional level, will empty one out more, and more to that point, which God alone can fulfil. 'You have made us for yourself, O Lord, and our hearts are restless until they rest in you.'[2]

Sadness visits the monk when his memory recalls all the goods and happiness that he has willingly left behind. He dreams of a house and family and above all he dreams of being acknowledged and loved.

But sometimes the sadness is too great, the desert too

[2]   St Augustine, *Confessions*, I, p. 1.

arid. He was looking for joy and found the Cross. What remedy is there for his sadness? He must rediscover the spirit of poverty. A rich person is someone who expects everything. A poor person is someone for whom everything is gift. Nothing is owed us, not even our existence. 'What do you have that you have not received?' Friendship, happiness, joy are not owed us.

The spirit of poverty should allow the monk to shoulder his burdens and frustrations (and hence become an adult), and to receive the simplest things as gifts: a ray of sunshine, a scrap of bread and some water. Little by little he will learn contentment. 'Desire all you have and you have all you desire!'

But this contentment is not yet joy. Joy is the experience in the depths of your being that the Transpersonal, the goal of all desire, dwells here and now. God Is. No one can rob you of this joy.

Obviously we are no longer speaking of something sensible, affective or rational, but of the ground of being. For the ancient monks, it is only when you can root your joy here that you can truly radiate joy in daily life.

This joy no longer depends on externals, on what happens to us. It is no longer a question of health or temperament but of fidelity to the uncreated Presence who dwells within each person. This is joy that abides. This joy is not the cheerfulness or lightheartedness of the privileged temperament, but the deep tranquillity of someone who encounters another not to fulfil his or her own needs but for the pleasure of communing with the life which at once unites and transcends them.

Listlessness (Akedia)

Sadder than sadness itself, *akedia* or listlessness is a particular form of the death instinct that introduces into all our actions disgust and lassitude. It leads to despair and at times to suicide. Today we would call this dejection or clinical depression. The desert monks called it the noonday devil and described with great precision this state in which the monk, after having known the spiritual consolations of starting out, begins to doubt his spiritual journey. It is the great doubt: Had he not after all been abused? What good has it served spending all this time in the desert? He no longer finds any pleasure in the liturgy or religious observances. God seems nothing more than a projection, a fantasy or a childish notion. Would it not be better, therefore, simply to abandon solitude altogether, to be of some use in the world, to do something? At times this noonday devil will incite this chaste and sober person to catch up on lost time especially in regard to sensuality and strong drink.

In his theory of individuation, C.G. Jung describes very accurately this moment of crisis, when a person in mid-life finds his or her whole life put into question. It is a time when repressed material can suddenly manifest itself with violence. But it can also mark a crucial moment of passage towards a deeper integration. The values of having are substituted for those of Being. From now on the person's life is no longer oriented towards the affirmation of the ego, but towards this ego taking second place and being integrated into that archetype of wholeness, which Jung called the Self.

It is a particularly difficult time. All the former supports and certainties fall by the wayside, and nothing seems to be taking the place of this collapsing edifice. If the person seeks help or consolation, it only heightens the despair, the feeling of complete unknowing to which one seems condemned.

For this affliction, the desert fathers counsel much prayer. One is capable of little else. Their suggestion of manual labour won't be of great relief. Nevertheless, it is necessary to occupy the mind with simple tasks and to live in the present moment without looking either to the past or to the future. The pain of each day suffices. It becomes a question of holding firm at the heart of the anguish. It is a time for fidelity. Loving God no longer means *feeling* that one loves God. It is enough to want to love God. It is also the entrance into the desert of faith. One believes because one wants to believe. The aid of reason is a crutch that has already been burnt in the fires of fatigue and doubt. It is the moment of greatest freedom, when one can either choose or reject God.

Was it this demon of *akedia* that took hold of Judas and Peter at the time of their betrayal? It conquered Judas and led him to despair and suicide. Judas doubted the mercy of God. But Peter conquered it by repentance.

The noonday devil can lead us to Hell in the sense that it can enclose us in ourselves. There is no longer a flaw or an opening for Love to enter.

Again the ancients remind us that this trial will pass. Sometimes it lasts longer than other trials, but like everything else it will pass. There is no unending pain, and the one who perseveres ought to know that this demon is not followed immediately by another. Peace and joy follow this battle.

Vainglory (Kenodoxia)

Vainglory or ego-inflation – it is the story of the frog that wanted to be as big as an ox. One finds ego-inflation at the root of paranoia (positive or negative). Without any basis whatever this 'I' fancies itself the object either of admiration or denigration. This sickness characteristically places the individual at the centre of the universe, like a child who demands everyone's attention and who is the standard for interpreting everything that happens. The 'I' demands absolute recognition in which all the shortcomings and frustrations of the past are overlooked. The bigger the sense of insecurity, the greater the need to boast of deeds accomplished and acquaintances made. All this reinforces a false sense of importance. The person becomes particularly irritable and vulnerable as soon as the lovely image which this 'I' has of itself is put into question. A simple remark and he or she feels hopelessly persecuted.

Merely crack a smile, and the whole world is singing the praises of this genius.

In the desert these caricatures present themselves under more subtle guises. But the problem is fundamentally the same. The 'I' usurps the prerogatives of the deeper self and plays God.

Evagrius tells us that a monk tortured by ego-inflation *thinks* he has actually become very spiritual indeed. He believes the beauty of his visions, the new records set by his fasts. How could he possibly doubt his sanity? Before long all the sick will come running to him. Sinners will come knocking at his door, and with a single glance of the eye he will convert them all.

In Evagrius's view, ego-inflation also makes the monk dream of becoming a priest. While perhaps surprising today, at that time the priesthood was vested with such dignity that any monk would deem himself unworthy of such a grace. To desire ordination was the height of presumption.

The antidote, according to Evagrius – we could still find this shocking – is knowledge. There is nothing like self-knowledge for being delivered from illusions.

Who are we really? A person is like grass. In the morning it flourishes and at night it withers and fades. What is this world? A drop of water in a bucket. Self-knowledge returns one to one's proper place as a creature. What did you have that you did not first receive? So why boast instead of giving thanks?

This knowledge is also knowledge of God, the knowledge of Being, which frees one by discerning the power of illusion. The angels are far humbler than humans because they are more intelligent. Vainglory is a failure to know not only oneself but also the Ultimate Reality, which makes all else relative to it. When self-knowledge sets us free from this demon of *kenodoxia*, we risk finding ourselves again tempted by grief (*lupé*) or boredom (*akedia*). One is no longer what one thought. To mourn the loss of these illusions is never painless. But better this than to be led gradually towards the madness which is pride. For just as lightning precedes thunder, so ego-inflation announces pride.

Pride (Hyperphania)

If the old monks considered ego-inflation to be a sign of stupidity or mental weakness, pride manifests an even deeper ignorance of human nature. Pride can effectively lead to the complete break with Reality characteristic of schizoid states. A person enclosed in self-satisfaction becomes entrapped in a sort of autistic world of fantasy with no hope of communication with the Other.

The philosophers, like the monks, spoke of *hybris* or excess as being the cause of all evils. Pride is a sort of excess on the spiritual level: a creature (who has no being of its own) assumes the rights and powers of the Creator. But the monks do not speculate about this; they describe the concrete situation. A proud person judges others as though he or she were God who alone searches the heart. A proud monk fancies himself the cause of his own existence, as though he could give himself life and breath. Pride can lead a person to aberration, to the point of being 'out of oneself'. The word Evagrius uses here is *ekstasis*. Ecstasy re-centres the person ever more deeply in God who is at once beyond and within. God is more other than myself and more me than I myself am.

If a proud monk is struck or gossiped about, he quickly loses his head and can even become wildly furious. A humble monk in the same situation will react very differently, as if the injury and calumny could not enter the peaceful core of his being. Being unpretentious, the humble person knows tranquillity and expects no sign of admiration from others for simply being himself. So the great remedy for pride is, according to the desert fathers, humility.

They are relentless on the therapeutic effects of this virtue. Humility is, simply, the truth. It is to be who you are, no more no less. It is to have no longer one's gaze directed towards God, no longer at oneself.

The word 'humility' comes from *humus*, meaning earth. To be humble is to accept one's earthy condition and to marvel at how this can be capable of thought and love – and God.

As for this demon of pride, the desert fathers recommend their monks to turn towards Christ, the perfect human, the archetype, the person we truly are, 'who, being in the form of God, did not count equality with God something to be grasped. But he emptied himself, taking the form of a slave, becoming as human beings are, he was humbler yet, even to accepting death, death on a cross. And for this God raised him high, and gave him the name which is above all other names' (Ph 2.6–9). This emptying or purification of our ego is revealed in us as a vastness that contains all things.

There are many other kinds of tormenting thoughts, but these are all derived from the eight principle ones. The ancients are not casuists but therapists. Their analysis of all these thoughts leads back to the root of suffering, so that we might be definitively free of them. This root is, in the language of Paul, the 'old self', the self that comforts itself by eating or avarice or pleasure, the self which gets furious when someone disagrees, the self which is saddened by what it lacks, despairs in boredom.

The desert fathers want to substitute this 'old self' of St Paul, a pathological ego-centred attitude, with the Christ- or God-centred one. In the psychological language of today we would speak of replacing the neurotic attitude of someone caught in the grip of self-images, with a non ego-centric attitude that is open to those adventures inspired by the awareness of life. I am not the only one alive – me and my memories, needs, shortcomings. There is also the Mystery of Life which flows in me with its plenitude, its generosity.

When we are no longer self-centred, no longer slaves of this infantile self who always has to be the centre of the universe and who sufffers terribly whenever deprived, we become capable of loving and serving without counting the cost. Is this not the natural, non-pathological way of the adult? It is true, nevertheless, that precious few attain this maturity.

'Grace,' said Bernanos, 'is to forget yourself.' This self-forgetfulness is not the result of a specific act of the will, but the fruit of an experience of transcendence at the heart of the ordinary. Seeing each thing as it is in itself, not simply as it relates to us, restores our clarity. It does not exile us from the world, it restores it. We return to the Real world, but we remain free with respect to it – 'in the world but not of the world'.

This state of *apatheia*, which we have described as a non-pathological state of being, is spontaneous, innocent, simple. *Apatheia* also describes the state of purity of heart, a capacity to love regardless of the circumstances. It is the love of enemies which Christ spoke of, a state of luminosity and lightness of the body itself. The transparence of the divine energies, as St Seraphim of Sarov, among others, showed us, gives the physical body the character of a luminous or resurrected body (think of the great theme of the Transfiguration and the Resurrection of the flesh in Christianity, the possibility of real participation of our body in divine life).

Chapter Four

A Hesychast in the West: St John Cassian

Along with Augustine of Hippo, John Cassian is one of the more important personalities in the Church at the beginning of the fifth century. He is considered an authoritative voice of the tradition, particularly the tradition which he received from St John Chrysostom and from the various desert fathers in Egypt and Syria.

When Gennadius composed his *On Illustrious Men*, he identified Cassian simply as 'Sanctus Cassianus', and many bishops of Rome have used the same term. In a letter to Abbess Respecta of Marseilles, Gregory the Great testified that her monastery had been dedicated 'in honour of St. Cassian'. Popes Urban V and Benedict XIV went so far as to say that his sanctity could not be doubted. Alongside these authorities Cassian's sanctity is attested to in the martyrologies of Gaul and Greece. The tradition is unanimous. His feast is celebrated in the East on 28 or 29 October and in the West, in the diocese of Marseilles, on 23 July, the day after the feast of Mary Magdalene.

Biographical Details

Despite the historical uncertainties surrounding Cassian's origins, we know from his own testimony that he was born around 365 into a wealthy and religious family.

Current opinion regarding his birthplace is divided between Scythia Minor (modern-day Dubrovnik) and rural Provence. Once he had completed his classical studies, Cassian, under the aegis of his friend Germanus, decided to become a monk. Together they travelled to Palestine where they entered a monastery in Bethlehem. Their curiosity probably led them to communities of monks in Palestine, Syria and perhaps even Mesopotamia, whose customs are described in his *Institutes*.

'After receiving the rudiments of the faith and profiting from it,' writes Cassian, 'we began to feel once more the desire for a higher perfection and we resolved to conquer incontinence in Egypt.'[1] Choosing to travel by sea, since it was faster and safer, they began at Thennesus, situated at one of the eastern mouths of the Nile (close to modern-day Damiette). On the advice of the Bishop of Panephysis, they visited some solitaries living on some small islands in a nearby salt marsh. Cassian gives us three of their names: Cheremon, Hesteros and Joseph.

Next they travelled along the coast to 'a place bordered on one side by the river and on the other by the vastness of the sea, and they formed an island uninhabitable by anyone but monks in search of solitude.'[2] There Cassian and Germanus first met Abba Piamun, to whom Cassian says he is indebted for the basic principles of the solitary life, which he soon studied in more depth at Scete.[3] They also met Abba Abraham, as told in Cassian's *Conference* 24. Desiring to venture further into the desert, Cassian and Germanus headed upstream to the solitude of Scete, where the water is tainted with the taste of tar. Here the community of the priest, Paphnutius, lived. It was the first foundation of Macarius, whom Cassian considered a great man.[4] But Paphnutius also won Cassian's admiration. 'Among the choirs of saints, pure stars which glimmered

[1] *Institutes*, preface, 4.
[2] *Conference* XI, 2–3.
[3] *Conference* XVIII, 16.
[4] *Conference* XIV, 4.

in the night of this world, we saw the blessed Paphnutius, from whom knowledge shone with brilliance.'[5]

Cassian and Germanus also visited the desert of Mitry, where they met Evagrius Ponticus. They returned to Bethlehem and then left for Constantinople, where they met St John Chrysostom. Without abandoning their monastic life, they allowed themselves to be ordained by Chrysostom, Germanus to the priesthood and Cassian to the diaconate.

The brilliance of Chrysostom's preaching and the beauty of his teaching left an indelible mark on Cassian. He loved him deeply. At the end of his life he said he learnt everything he knew from Chrysostom. Nevertheless, caught up in the doctrinal and political conflicts which pitted a certain Theophilus against Chrysostom, who was Patriarch of Constantinople, Cassian was forced into exile. He made his way to Rome and, according to some accounts, became a friend of the future Pope, St Leo the Great. It was likewise at Rome that Cassian was ordained priest.

Cassian journeyed after these experiences to Marseilles around 415, where he founded two monasteries, one for men, the other for women.[6] Both the monks living in community and those living as solitaries asked him to become their spiritual father. Despite his taste for solitude and silence, he took on this burden without hesitation.

The important role he played in the disputes on grace shows his concern for tradition. 'Do not let yourselves be frightened when you intend to speak of virtue and do not make a monster out of this word. Virtue is not far from us; it does not dwell outside of us; it is enough to will ... The soul has been created good and in perfect uprightness it conforms itself to nature when it remains what it is ... We guard our souls for the Lord, like a deposit received from Him, so that he might recognize his work, while seeing it as he created it.'[7] Cassian is well situated in the tradition

5   *Conference* III, 1.
6   See Gennadius, *De viris illustribus*, 62.
7   St Athanasius, *Life of St Anthony*, 20.

which says that a bird needs two wings to fly: grace and nature. Augustine, anticipating Luther, had written that no one could do anything without God's grace. Cassian, following Athanasius, knew that nature needed to co-operate as well. St John Damascene would say later that 'conversion is a return to nature, from what is contrary to nature to what is proper to it'.

The Beginnings of Monastic Life

Cassian says that 'every art, every discipline has its own particular goal and an end proper to it; whoever seriously wants to excel, gives oneself ceaselessly and in light of this suffers all hardships, dangers and losses.'[8]

Cassian's Latin translates two Greek words: '*telos*' and '*skopos*'. According to the Stoics, '*telos*' means a reward, and '*skopos*' a race in a stadium. But in lexicons one generally finds the same meaning for both words: goal, end. Cassian, however, distinguishes the two terms. '*Telos*' is the final goal, and '*skopos*' is the path which permits attainment of the goal. To make himself better understood, Cassian places some comparisons in the mouth of Abba Moses. 'Behold the ploughman, braving in turn the rays of the scorching sun, then the cold and the ice. He breaks up the unyielding earth, tirelessly turning it again and again with the aid of a plough. He is faithful to the ultimate purpose of ridding it of brambles and making the soil by dint of labour as fine and loose as sand. He does not consider obtaining his end in any other way, that is, an abundant harvest by which he may live from now on, sheltered from necessity or even increase his wealth. He is seen emptying his baskets of grain out of the goodness of his heart and with intense labour he entrusts the seeds to the soft furrows. The prospect of future crops makes him impervious to the present loss. Consider also those who engage in trade as though they do not fear encountering

8   *Conference* I, 2.

the hazards of the sea. They take to the sky on the wings of hope. It is their goal.

'Those who embrace a military career are similar. They burn with ambition, and the distant prospects of honour and power blind them to the dangers and to the thousand deaths of the long journeys. Neither sufferings nor wars succeed in defeating them, because of the grandeur they so desire to obtain.'[9]

Whether it is the ploughman, the tradesman or the soldier, Cassian's attitude is the same: it is necessary to know what you want before setting out to do it. In the spiritual life, 'our profession', the same process is at work: 'It also has its goal and specific end, and to obtain it we endure every obstacle we meet without losing heart – better still, with joy. Neither fasts nor hunger tire us. We find pleasure in the fatigue of vigils. Diligent reading and meditation upon Scripture are never enough. The incessant labour, the nakedness, being stripped of everything, even the horror of this infinite solitude, do not terrify. It is this same end, without doubt, which made you forsake the love of your family, the sun of the homeland, the delights of the world and cross over many countries in order to go looking for the company of people who are like us, boorish and ignorant, lost amidst the desolate skies of this desert. Tell me, what is the purpose, what is the goal which leads you to tolerate so lightheartedly all these trials?'[10] Cassian and Germanus reply, 'It is the Kingdom of Heaven.' For the ancients, the Kingdom of Heaven is the Holy Spirit ruling over our faculties, 'on earth as it is in heaven', for it is one and the same Spirit who dwells in God and in us. The Kingdom is also the reign of love, love that informs and directs the other faculties.

The ancient monks often asked, 'What rules us?' The past? Memories? Ambition? Remorse? Desires? What *should* rule over us is love, 'for the person who abides in

9   *Conference* I, 2.
10   *Conference* I, 2.

love abides in God'. God's Spirit, God's energy, rules over us. The Kingdom is finally the sovereignty and power of Christ, 'who is all in all' – Light inaccessible taking flesh.

But what is the way to the Kingdom? What is the *skopos*, the method for arriving at this goal? For Cassian it is the purification of the heart. Without purity of heart the reign of God cannot establish itself in us. 'The purpose of our profession, as we have said, consists in the Kingdom of God or the Kingdom of Heaven; it is true. But our goal (that is, the way we get there) is purity of heart, without which it is impossible for anyone to attain the final goal. Fixing our gaze, therefore, on this goal, in order to set our course, we run straight ahead, like a neatly drawn line. If our mind wanders a bit, we can return to it again and use it as a standard by which to guide ourselves. This norm will draw on all our efforts to converge on this single point and will not fail to warn us immediately if our minds should veer off the proposed course.'[11]

One also finds in Cassian that distinction, so dear to Evagrius, between knowledge and ascetic practice.

The goal of the Christian life is knowledge, the vision of God, participation in the life of the Trinity, the reign of Being-Love. The method is ascetic practice, the purification of the passions and thoughts (*logismoi*), the purification of the heart. The purpose of ascetic practice is to purify the mind and heart and free them from the passions. He enjoys describing the difficulties one can meet along this path of liberation. Small things can be as big a hindrance as attachment to great things. Attachment to such subtle things as spiritual practices, doctrines, feelings, consolation is as much an impediment to freedom as attachment to wealth, reputation or food.

Those who forget to guard the mirror of the heart, who become attached to fleeting images and reflections, will never come to that pure light. But purity of heart is never

[11] *Conference* I, 4.

acquired once and for all. Each morning one must clean the mirror.

'Many who had given up considerable fortunes, enormous sums of gold and silver as well as magnificent estates, have allowed themselves to be upset by a scraper, a needle or a biro. If they had constantly maintained purity of heart, they would never have fallen for such trifling things after stripping themselves of extremely precious goods.

'There are some who are so jealous of a book that they cannot bear anyone else to look at it or touch it. Such an encounter, instead of gaining them the reward of gentleness and love, becomes for them an occasion for impatience and even death. After giving away all their riches for love of Christ, they take back their ancient passion and use it for worthless things and for whose sake they grow angry. They do not have the love of which Paul spoke, and their lives are stricken with complete sterility. The blessed Apostle foresaw this sadness: "if I give away all my possessions to buy food for the poor and give my body over to be burnt, but have not love, then it is for nothing" (1 Co 13.3). This is proof that perfection is not suddenly achieved just by being naked, or by renouncing riches and rejecting honours, unless one includes that love whose components the Apostle described. This love is purity of heart. For to know not jealousy, pride, anger, heedless behaviour; nor to seek what does not belong to one, nor delight in what is wrong; not to plan evil and the rest: what are these things other than to offer continually to God a perfect and pure heart, a heart kept free of the movement of passion?'[12]

This search for purity of heart is not only the search for paradise lost, for lost innocence, a return to the integrity of our true nature, it is also the search for the Kingdom, in the sense that love purifies everything – it is the alchemist's stone that transforms our base metal into gold.

[12] *Conference* I, 6.

'Purity of heart, then, will be the sole end of our actions and desires. It is for such purity that we must embrace solitude, endure fasts, vigils, work, nakedness, devote ourselves to reading and to the practice of other virtues for no other purpose than to render our hearts pure and guard them against every evil passion, and to climb, as by so many steps, to the perfection of charity.'[13]

Martha and Mary

After describing the goal of monastic life, Cassian insists on illustrating it with the gospel story that depicts Martha agitated in her concern over serving well, while her sister remained seated at Jesus' feet. 'This should be the primary focus of our efforts, the unswerving intention and constant desire of our hearts: to adhere always to God and to the things of God. Everything that diverts us from this path, however impressive, must be regarded as secondary, of little worth and a clear danger. In this spirit and manner of acting, the Gospel gives us a most beautiful example in the persons of Martha and Mary. It was a sacred ministry that Martha did in looking after the Lord and his disciples. Mary, however, attentive solely to spiritual teaching, remained at the feet of Jesus, which she covered with kisses and anointed with the perfume of her generous faith. But it is she whom the Lord prefers because she chose the better part, which cannot be taken away from her.'[14]

In language similar to that of Evagrius, Cassian says that Mary represents knowledge or contemplation, and Martha represents the active life of ascetic practice. The two sisters are inseparable, like 'two cheeks on the same face'. But one must remember that the goal of the active life is contemplation. It is this that remains 'the better part that will not be taken away'.

---

[13] *Conference* I, 7.
[14] *Conference* I, 8.

'So the toil of fasting and assiduous reading, the works of mercy, justice, devotion and hospitality will be taken from us and will not remain as we remain?'[15]

The abba to whom Cassian posed this question said that practise of the active life is in time, whereas contemplative knowledge is in eternity. We are in time. We practise the active life in time, knowing that our goal is in eternity. The role of the contemplative is to remind us that there is in the world something other than the world, that the goal of human life is beyond the human. Contemplation is the goal and meaning of work just as Sabbath is the goal and meaning of the weekdays.

With respect to action and contemplation, one should never oppose one to the other. What Jesus asks of Martha is that she love in her service, as Mary loved in her meditation. Everything one does without love is time wasted; everything one does with love is eternity regained.

Unceasing Prayer

In order to remain in that state of watchfulness and love, Cassian, following the desert fathers, reminds us that we have no other recourse than perpetual prayer. To pray without ceasing and to be pure of heart are one and the same happiness which permits the vision of God, that is, experiencing in our own limited way something of God's unlimited love. 'The entire purpose of the monk and the perfection of his heart consist in the uninterrupted perseverence in prayer. To the extent that this is possible for a fragile human, the monk strives for unstirring tranquillity of soul and perpetual purity.'[16]

This 'tranquillity of soul' is what the Greeks call '*hesychia*'. It is the fruit of prayer and purity of heart.

To arrive at this perpetual prayer or at this 'state of prayer', Cassian (much like the monks of Mount Athos

[15] *Conference* I, 9.
[16] *Conference* IX, 2.

later) suggests the use of a short phrase by which the mind can gather itself. 'It is a secret which has been taught to us by some of the oldest of the Fathers, and we pass it on only to a small number of souls who are truly eager to know it. To keep the thought of God ever in your mind you must say without ceasing this formula of piety: "O God, come to my assistance. O Lord, make haste to help me."

'It is not without reason that this short verse has been chosen out of the whole of Scripture. It expresses all the feelings of which human nature is capable. It can be adapted quite happily to every condition and can be used against every temptation.

'It carries within it a cry to God for help in the face of every danger. It is a humble and pious confession. It bears both the vigilance of a soul forever on guard against fear as well as a sense of our frailty. It expresses the confidence of being heard and the assurance of help that is always and everywhere present. For anyone who continually invokes his protector is most certain of having him nearby. It is the voice of love and of burning charity; it is the cry of the soul who keeps an eye out for traps and trembles in the face of the enemy; it is the cry of someone who is attacked night and day and exclaims that he cannot escape unless his protector comes to his aid.'[17]

Isn't this an excellent description of what will later be called 'prayer of the heart'?

The energy contained in this short invocation from person to person, is what Cassian calls a 'well-guarded secret'.

While meditating on these conferences, we might discover for ourselves the different elements and signs that accompany deep prayer (tears, fire, humility, joy). These signs are still too much in the realm of feeling, still too self-conscious. We must go beyond them, let go of them. For prayer is not perfect, said Anthony, when the monk is aware of himself and knows that he is praying.

---

[17] *Conference* X, 10.

A Path of Joy

If Cassian often speaks of repentence and awareness of faults, he equally insists upon the joy of the monks. They are happy people, 'people of celebration'. They are no longer of this world, which is the 'the kingdom of sadness and despair'. Their kingdom is Joy and Peace in the Holy Spirit. 'The coming of the kingdom of God,' says the Evangelist, 'does not admit of observation and there will be no one to say, "Look, it is here! Look, it is there!" For look, the kingdom of God is among you' (Lk 17.20–21). But in us there can only be either knowledge or ignorance of the truth or love of virtue or of vice, and out of these we make a kingdom in the heart either for the devil or for Christ. The Apostle, in his turn, describes the kingdom: "For it is not eating and drinking that make the kingdom of God, but the saving justice, the peace and the joy brought by the Holy Spirit" (Rm 14.17). If, then, the kingdom of God is within us, and it consists of justice, of peace and of joy, then whoever lives in these virtues is without doubt in the Kingdom of God; and whoever lives, on the other hand, in injustice, discord and death-dealing gloom, is subject to the kingdom of the devil, of hell, of death; for it is by these signs that the two kingdoms are discerned.'[18]

When he speaks of 'unshaken tranquillity and unending joy', Cassian seems to fear that we take him for some sort of utopian dreamer, or worse, that we accuse him of hedonism. That is why he makes it quite clear that this is a 'joy and a peace that the world cannot give' and not an anti-depressant. Following the Apostle, he specifies that it concerns joy in the Holy Spirit, which is different from that joy about which is written, 'woe to you who laugh because you will cry'. This joy transcends opposites and does not depend on pleasant encounters or favourable circumstances. It is the joy of Being. Laughter, cheerfulness, good humour do not approach this joy which abounds even in

---

[18] *Conference* I, 13.

the midst of tribulation; it is ontological joy, the heart's opening onto another awareness.

Cassian tells us we are capable of this unique joy, the fruit of unceasing prayer and of trust in God, and he insists we remember what is held out to us in Scripture: 'I want you to have some other guarantee of the truth of my words other than my own conjecture, the authority of the Lord Himself. Listen to Him as he paints a most illuminating picture of the nature and conditions of the world to come. "Look! I am creating a new heaven and a new earth. Former things will be forgotten; they will no longer live in the secret of the heart. But you will delight and rejoice forever in these things which I bring forth." Or again, "Joy and happiness will be found in this; worship and songs of praise month after month, from Sabbath to Sabbath." Yet again, "Joy and gladness will be their portion; pain and sighing will take flight." If you desire something clearer regarding the life and city of the saints, listen to the voice of the Lord as He speaks to the heavenly Jerusalem: "I will give you peace as a visitor and justice will judge you. Iniquity shall no longer be heard of in your country nor ravage and ruin within your borders. Salvation will hold your walls and praise will be at your gates. No more will the sun illumine your day, and the splendour of the moon will not shine upon you. You shall have the Lord for your everlasting light and your God for your glory. Your sun will set no more, and your moon will not diminish. The Lord will be an everlasting light for you, and the days of your mourning will come to an end".'[19]

Like a sun that never sets is the heart which roots itself in Love through prayer and, in the image of Living Justice and Mercy, shines on the just and unjust alike. It knows the peace (*hesychia, quies*) of one who has nothing other to do but love. Pilgrim and voyager along the winding paths of obscurity, he remains in the light, and many rejoice in his brightness.

[19] *Conference* I, 13.

Chapter Five

Apophasis and Fatherhood in Early Christianity and in Hesychasm

It is better to say that God does not exist than to project onto the Infinite our needs and fantasies. The fourth-century bishop, Gregory of Nyssa (c. 332–395) says that 'every concept formed by our understanding which attempts to attain and to hem in the divine nature serves only to make an idol of God, not to make God known.'[1] In much the same spirit, Dostoyevsky says that the atheist is sometimes closer to God than the believer who knows nothing of God except the ideas and images he or she has been taught.

The apophatic way, with its unrelenting lucidity, is not unaware of this. Its slow work of deconstructing ideas and idols leads to the naked experience of the Real, to the divinization of humanity and the cosmos, to the intelligent childhood that plays in astonishment with the spatio-temporal elements of the Divine Comedy.

We will study this apophatic tradition in ancient Christianity and in its biblical roots in order to observe that it is not merely Platonic speculation. Apophasis is something lived, and the biblical metaphors of the night and the desert, taken up by mystics of every age, are apt.

[1] *The Life of Moses*, II, 165.

The hesychastic tradition affirms the transcendence of God and our real sharing in the life of Christ. The people who embody this tradition are the starsky, the *gerontes*, or spiritual fathers.

The Apophatic Tradition

No one has ever seen God, St John tells us (John 1.18). St Paul adds that God lives in inaccessible Light, whom no one has seen or can see (1 Timothy 6.16). First-century Christians, faithful to these words, are prudent when they speak of God. At this time there is no Christian theology in the modern sense of the term. A theologian is above all 'one who prays', who celebrates. He gives no discourse on God. He sings and praises God, participating even in the life of the Son and the Spirit who cry in him: *Abba–Father*. But as St Justin Martyr († *c.* 165) recalls, the terms 'Father, God, Creator, Lord ... are not divine names: they are names drawn form his benefits and his works.'[2] The names of God which we use (Father, Creator, etc.) do not describe God in the sense of defining him. Rather they gesture towards God and point to him from afar.

The word 'God' itself, *Deus* in Latin, means 'luminous day'. It is a symbol of Light which illumines all things but remains invisible. St Hilary of Poitier (315–367) adds: 'God is invisible, ineffable, infinite. Words fail to describe God. The mind falters in its search. In trying to grasp, the intelligence finds no place to grasp.'[3]

If apophasis reminds us of the symbolic character of language, it likewise fashions for itself its own proper language which abounds in negative terms: invisible, ineffable, infinite, uncreated, inaccessible. Thus, St Thomas will say, 'Concerning God, one cannot say what God is, but only what God is not.' In this manner the apophatic way recalls the transcendence of God, that divine other-

---

[2]   *Apology*, II.
[3]   *De trinitate*, II, 6.

ness which neither the mind, nor the senses nor anything created can grasp.

It is God as completely Other, a different Nature. God's incomprehensibility is not simply due to the limitations and weakness of our instruments of comprehension. It is God's very Nature.

'Concerning God it is impossible to say what God is in Himself; it is more precise to speak of God by negations. God is not, in fact, another thing. This is not to say tht God does not exist, but that God is above all that is, beyond being itself.'[4] St John Damascene is joined by a number of contemporary theologians who refuse, with Heidegger, to consider God as Essence or as Being. God would then be bound to the perishable fate of metaphysics and ontology.[5] God is more than being.

Some, like Meister Eckhart and Jacob Boehme, go so far as to say that God is 'a pure Nothing', thus making nothingness the pre-condition and origin of being. 'Being is nothing but a small blemish on the purity of Non-Being', as Paul Valéry says. But these words are traps. They become the source of intrigue and inquisition, if not an outright battle of words.

The 'Nothingness' of which the gnostics speak is above all the 'naughting' (in the sense of purification) of all our ways of thinking and acting. God is the Beyond-Everything (as Gregory of Nazianzus says), the Beyond Being.

No one can see God without abandoning the ways we idolize God. To be reduced to nothing, to consent to the emptiness and unknowing, is to produce in ourselves the womb of true knowledge, which will make us – in the language of Eckhart – 'mothers of God'.

The writings of (Pseudo) Denys in this area have influenced many, especially in the Middle Ages. St John of the Cross and Carmelite mysticism were also strongly influenced by this unknown author who took the name Denys

---

4 St John Damascene, *On the Orthodox Faith*, I, 4.
5 See Jean-Luc Marion, *Dieu sans l'être*, Paris, 1982.

the Areopagite, disciple of St Paul and first bishop of Athens. Here are but a few important texts.

'To celebrate the negations ... in order to know without veils this unknowing which itself is concealed from every being that has knowledge, in order to see this superessential darkness that hides all light contained in beings.'[6]

'If it should happen that, seeing God, one begins to comment on what one sees, it is because one has not seen God himself, but one of those things which one ought to be able to know about God. For in himself God is beyond all being and knowing; and because God is beyond being and knowing, God is and is known only in so far as he is completely unknown and non-existent. This perfect unknowing, taken in the best sense of the word, constitutes true knowledge of God who is beyond all knowledge.'[7]

'We say, therefore, that the universal Cause, which transcends the entire universe, is neither matter ... nor has a body. It has neither figure nor form nor quality nor mass. It is in no particular place and cannot be grasped by the senses.... Climbing yet higher, we now say that this Cause has neither soul nor intelligence; ... that one can neither express it nor conceive of it; that it has neither number, nor order, nor greatness nor smallness, neither equality nor inequality, neither similarity nor dissimilarity. It neither remains still nor moves.... It has neither power nor light. It is neither living nor not living. It is neither essence, perpetuity, nor time. One cannot grasp it intellectually. It is not knowledge, truth, kingship, wisdom, one, unity, divinity or good. It is not spirit or sonship or paternity in a way we can understand. No is it anything which is accessible to our knowledge or to the knowledge of any other being; nor has it anything that pertains to being. Nor one knows it as it is.... It escapes our power to reason, name and know. It is neither dark nor light, neither true nor

6   *The Mystical Theology*, II.
7   Letter I to Gaius.

false. One can affirm or deny nothing of it. When we make affirmations and denials that relate to inferior things, we affirm or deny nothing of this Cause. For every affirmation remains on this side of its transcendence, which is deprived of everything and is beyond everything.'[8]

Let us summarize these illogical and paradoxical phrases which characterize the apophatic style. God has no name and God has every name. God is none of the things that exist and God is everything. One knows God only through not knowing. Every affirmation, like every negation, remains on this side of God's transcendence. 'God is the Mystery, who is beyond even God, the Ineffable, whom all things name; complete affirmation, complete negation; beyond every affirmation and beyond every negation.'[9]

Hence, the apophatic way is not simply a negative theology. Ultimate Reality is beyond both negation and affirmation, that is, beyond the dual operation of the mind: neither this nor that.

Apophasis is the direct apprehension of the Real just as it is, without the projections of the discursive mind that distort the Real. It is to see without eyes, to comprehend without the mind. And if it is only 'like that knows like', it is necessary to become God in order to know God. As the Evangelist says, 'we shall be like him, because we shall see him as he really is' (1 Jn 3.2).

The texts of Denys strike us as mere speculation if we remove them from the existential, biblical context in which they are rooted. The God of the Bible is in fact a hidden God (Isaiah 45.15). He has made darkness his hiding place (Psalm 17.12), and one can interpret the sacred tetra-gramma, YHWH, the unutterable name revealed to Moses at the Burning Bush, as God's refusal to name himself. 'I am who am. Go, walk in my Presence; you will see who I am, who I will be ....'

The path of apophatic ascent, where one gradually

---

8   *The Mystical Theology*, IV–V.
9   *The Divine Names*, II, 4.

loosens one's grip on all that is known, is likened by Denys (as by many others, such as Gregory of Nyssa) to the ascent of Moses on Mount Sinai. 'Letting go of that world where one sees and is seen, Moses entered into the truly mystical darkness of unknowing: here he silenced all positive knowledge; here he entirely escaped vision's grasp, for he belonged entirely to God, who is beyond everything, and no longer to himself or to anything else. He is united by what is better in himself to God who escapes all knowledge, having renounced all positive knowledge, and, by the grace of this unknowing, even knowing beyond all intelligence.'[10]

It should thus be clear that the path upon which Denys invites us, following Moses, does not lead to 'Nothing' but through 'Nothing' to Union. The goal of the apophatic way, according to Denys, is ecstasy, supreme happiness, union with the living God, which even terms such as Being, Pure Act (Aristotle), the One (Plotinus) cannot describe.

'It is a good thing to speak of God,' said Gregory of Nazianzus, 'but it is better to purify oneself for God.' The apophatic way is, therefore, a practical way which leads to ecstasy. The desert for the monks, the night for the mystics, will be the crucibles wherein one realizes the incomprehensible Union of the Created and Uncreated.

Christ is not forgotten along this way. He is himself the Way, the One in whom the union of opposites is achieved, the paradoxical Unity of the human person and God, of finite and Infinite, of created and Uncreated. He is the archetype in time and in Eternity, of what is God in humans and of what is human in God.

'In the humanity of Christ,' affirms Denys the Areopagite, 'the Superessential manifests itself to the human essence without ceasing to remain hidden after this manifestation or, to express myself in a more divine

---

[10] *The Mystical Theology*, 1, 3; see also Gregory of Nyssa, *The Life of Moses*, I, 46.

manner, is hidden at the heart of the manifestation. The person remains in the mystery because the mystery of Jesus remains hidden. No reason or understanding can exhaust who God is in Himself. What one can say of God is that he is ineffable. What one can know of God is that he is unknowable.'[11]

Christ is the Eternal Master incarnated in space and time. He is the Visible and the Invisible, the Teaching of the Hidden Master.

Hesychasm

Proceeding directly from this apophatic tradition, hesychasm will be profoundly Christocentric. Without Christ, in fact, divinization is not possible. Christ's incarnation establishes the full communion between God and humanity. God became human so that humans might become God. 'God became the bearer of flesh so that humanity might become the bearer of the Spirit,' said Athanasius of Alexandria.

This is the refrain of all the Fathers of the Church: the presence of Christ in the world does not abolish the apophatic way; on the contrary, it deepens it.

'The incarnation is a mystery more inconceivable than any other. In taking on human flesh, God made Himself understood only by appearing even more incomprehensible. God remains hidden even in this self-manifestation. Even while making Himself known, God remains ever unknown.'[12]

Simone Weil says, 'The incarnation of Christ does not dispel the mystery; it deepens it.' That God is incomprehensible is easy to accept. That this incomprehensible God loves us and becomes incarnate in space and time goes beyond reason.

'Christ unites in love created reality and uncreated

[11] Letter III.
[12] Maximus the Confessor, *Ambigua 5*.

reality and shows that by virtue of this grace the two are but one thing. The entire world enters completely into the totality of God and, becoming everything God is, except the divine nature itself, it receives in place of itself the fullness of God.'[13]

According to our baptismal commitment, the Christian life is not one of simply following a moral code, it is to unite in ourselves the two natures, human and divine, created and uncreated, that the two might become one *so that the world might believe.*

This paradoxical union, which is realized in the Spirit, recreates us in the image and likeness of the Son of God. Humanity rediscovers the beauty for which it was created.

This union also leads the hesychasts to affirm with Gregory of Palamas the reality of the experience of God, while continuing to affirm His transcendence. Hence, Gregory of Palamas says, 'Because the faithful can participate in God and because God's superessential essence cannot be shared in, there is some link between this essence which cannot be shared in and the faithful that allows them to participate in God. And if you suppress this – oh what a tragedy – you separate us from God, and, in destroying this link, you create an enormous, unbridgeable chasm between God, on the one hand, and the creation and rule over all creatures, on the other. It would be necessary to find another God who possessed in himself not only his own end, his own energy and deification, but also one who was Goodness (for it would not suffice for this God to exist merely for the contemplation of himself); not just perfect, but beyond all fullness. Thus, when he wanted in his goodness to do something good, he could. He would not only be immobile but could also put himself in motion. This way God would be present to all through his manifestations and his creative, providential energies. In a word, we would have to find a God in whose life we could share in one way or another, so that each of

---

[13] Maximus the Confessor, *Ambigua* 41.

us might receive being, life and deification in the manner most suited to each by way of participation.'[14]

Gregory of Palamas (1296–1359) continues in the tradition of the Cappadocians, of Denys the Areopagite, and of Maximus the Confessor.

'One can truly say that "the pure in heart see God", and that no one has ever seen God. Indeed, he who is invisible by nature becomes visible through his works.'[15]

'We affirm that we know God in his works, but we can hardly expect to approach the divine essence itself; for God's essence remains inaccessible, whereas God's energies come to us.'[16]

'We can partake of God only in so far as God communicates himself to us, but of God's ineffable essence we may never partake.'[17]

Though we can participate in God, truly experience God, God is at the same time impassible and ever beyond what we can understand or contain. God at once fulfils desire and forever empties it. The Christian never arrives, never gets full of God. The Christian remains a being of desire, someone living. It is precisely what this beautiful text of Gregory of Nyssa expresses so well: 'The unbounded, incomprehensible divine reality remains beyond all comprehension. Thus, the great David, placing his ascents in his heart, and advancing "from strength to strength" (Ps 83.7), cried out to God: "You are the Most High forever, Lord" (Ps 91.8). By this I think he means that from the endless ages of eternity, the person who runs towards you becomes ever greater and more exalted, while always progressing through the increase of grace. "You are the same, you remain the Most High forever" (Ps 101.13) . . . .

'That which is grasped at each moment is indeed

---

[14] Gregory of Palamas, *Triads*, III, 2.

[15] Gregory of Nyssa, *Homilies on the Beatitudes*, 6.

[16] Basil of Caesarea, Letter 234.

[17] Maximus the Confessor, cited by Euthyme Zigabene, *Dogmatic Panoply* 3.

greater than what he had attained before, but because what is sought has no limit, the limit of what has been discovered becomes for those who ascend a beginning for another discovery of higher realities. Thus the person who rises never stops, going from one beginning to another beginning by means of beginnings which never end. The person who ascends never lets desire remain in what is already known; rather, elevating himself by an ever greater desire, he pursues his path into the infinite by ascending ever higher.'[18]

To Hand on Unknowing is to Hand on an Experience

Two affirmations characterize hesychastic experience: the affirmation of divine transcendence, of God's inaccessible essence, and the nearness of God, God's immanence and presence in each of us, the divinization of humanity through the energies of the Word and the Spirit.

These two affirmations characterize the starsky or *gerontes* of whom the tradition speaks and such as we know even today on Mount Athos, for it is a tradition that still lives.

These wise figures are more humble than most because they are more intelligent. Being closer to the infinite and ineffable, they see their limitations and ignorance. Their humility is tied to this 'unknowing' with respect to the divine nature. At the same time the presence of God is something one can experience even in the flesh, as Motovilov would see at the feet of Master Seraphim.

If I were to say 'I know God', I would be a liar. God is beyond comprehension. Better to be silent and live in humility. If I were to say, 'I do not know God', I would also be a liar.

One finds examples of this double bind in the numerous tale of that collection of deeds and sayings known as the *Paterika* or the *Apophthegmata Patrum*.

---

[18] Gregory of Nyssa, *Homilies on the Song of Songs*, 8.

First on humility: 'A young man went in search of a spiritual father to teach him the way of perfection, but the old man said not a word. The young man asked the reason for his silence: "Am I some sort of superior who tells you what to do?" said the old man. "I'm not saying a word. If you want, do what you see me doing."'

In his book, *Witness of Beauty*, Paul Evdokimov offers this comment: 'A spiritual father is never a "director of conscience". He never begets *his* spiritual child; rather he engenders a child of God, mature and free. The disciple then receives the charism of spiritual attentiveness; the father receives the charism of being an instrument of the Holy Spirit. In this case every act of obedience is obedience to the will of God, while at the same time sharing in the acts of the obedient Christ.'[19]

The relationship of master to disciple becomes rather like participating in the spirit of love between the Father and the Son. Obedience, humility and mutual gift are not merely virtues, but the imitation of divine life.

'An old man said, "Many have imprudently overtaxed their bodies and have gone off without discovering anything. We have fasted until it hurts; we know the Scriptures by heart; we recite the psalms, but we do not have what God is looking for: love and humility."'[20]

This humility leads to love, which is the distinctive quality of the spiritual parent. St Isaac the Syrian says to his disciple, 'Listen, my brother, to the commandment I enjoin on you: let mercy ever increase in your scales until you feel in yourself the mercy with which God tests the world.'

Or, 'St Paissius the Great used to pray for his disciple who had denied Christ. Once when he was praying the Lord appeared to him saying: "Paissius, for whom are you praying?" But the saint did not stop praying for his disciple, and finally the Lord said, "Paissius, have you become

[19] Paul Evdokimov, *Témoins de la beauté*, Contacts, 1971, p. 159.
[20] *Apophthegmata Patrum*, Anonymous Series, 90.

one with me through your love?"'

'A spiritual person,' says Gregory of Nazianzus, 'is an agent of divine love.' And once again St Isaac, 'The spiritual person's heart is aflame with love for every creature, even for reptiles and demons.'

Abba Poemen refuses to punish and shows the maternal aspect of fatherhood, 'When I see a brother who has dozed off during prayer, I place his head on my knees and let him rest.' It is written of Abba Macarius the Great that he became a sort of terrestrial god because, just as God protects the world, Abba Macarius covered the mistakes he saw as though he had not seen them, the mistakes he heard as though he had not heard them.

'Question: when do you know that your heart has become pure? Response: when you consider all people to be good, and when no one seems impure or defiled to you, then you are truly pure of heart.'[21]

Above and beyond the characteristics of humility and love, proper to any true spiritual master, hesychasm adds the experience of light and certitude.

Symeon the New Theologian (942–1022), a Studite monk and abbot of the Monastery of St Mamas in Constantinople, occupies an exceptional place in the history of Eastern Christian spirituality. He is not afraid to confront traditional institutions in the Church with the spiritual experience of the mystical life. Some of his positions seem to run counter to the sense of humility and apophasis of which we have spoken earlier. It is simply another aspect of the incomprehensibility of God.

Inaccessible, God makes himself accessible in his love for us. God divinizes the one who, in ignorance and unknowing, abandons himself to God. 'Whoever does not know God in this life,' says St Symeon, 'will not know God in the next.' Symeon insists on the necessity of spiritual experience, particularly for those who act as guides. 'Whoever has not received the Baptism of the Spirit is

---

[21] Isaac the Syrian, *Ascetical Treatises*, 85.

not born into the spiritual life. In the order of grace, such a person falls from existence and is incapable of anything, not least engendering spiritual children, since he himself has not been born.'[22]

True Prayer

Western Catholic culture will be surprised at the place hesychasm gives to the body and the senses. Indeed, in contrast to the dualistic tendencies of hellenism, matter and the body are not to be held in contempt, but transfigured. The body is not the tomb of the soul, but, as St Paul says, the temple of the Holy Spirit (I Corinthians 6.19).

The Gospel does not oppose matter to spirit, nor body to soul, but it does contrast the Uncreated and created. The human spirit is radically different from God, but God, in bestowing grace, completely saves it.

Because of the Incarnation, our bodies have become temples of the Holy Spirit and it is here in the body that we must manifest the Glory of God. The purpose of the sacraments, especially the Eucharist, is not only to bring healing but also to immerse us in the divine-human nature of Christ.

Thus Symeon the New Theologian can say, 'The one who communes with divine grace is no longer alone but entirely in you, Oh Christ. . . . By myself I am but straw, but miraculously I feel myself suddenly inflamed like the Burning Bush of old. . . . Lord, you have granted that this corruptible temple be united to your sacred flesh, and that my blood mix with yours, and from now on I am part of you, transparent and transluscent.'[23]

This experience of the Spirit in the body is the experience of Mount Tabor where uncreated light was made visible in the body of Christ. The apostles only benefited from the exterior dimension of the Transfiguration

[22] I. Hausherr, *Vie par Nicetas Stétathos*, lxx.
[23] *Discourses*, 95.

because Christ had not yet died and risen. But now we are capable of discovering this light of Mount Tabor.

'Why did he not illumine those who worthily commune with the divine ray of his body which is in us, while illumining their being just as he will illumine the bodies of disciples on Tabor? Because this body, source of light and grace, was not yet united to our bodies: it illumined exteriorly those who worthily approached and sent forth light to the soul through the eyes. But today, because he is identified with us and exists in us, he illumines the soul only from within.'[24]

The experience of the Transfiguration or the vision of uncreated light characterizes the great orthodox masters. But how does one hand on this experience? In humility and love, but also with all the power of certitude. This is the testimony of the nineteenth-century Motovilov who asked the great Seraphim of Sarov (1759–1833), 'How can I be certain of being in the Spirit of God? How can I recognize unmistakeably within myself God's manifestation?'

At first Seraphim did not reply with words. He shared his own experience of light. This is the transmission of knowledge: the entrance into participation in a Presence that envelops the soul and the body. Then Seraphim said, 'My friend, we are both right now in the Spirit of God.... Why can't you look at me?'

'I can't look at you, Father. Your eyes are like flashes of lightning, and your face shines like the sun, and it hurts my eyes to look at you.'

'Have no fear,' he said, 'for you have now become as bright as I am. You are also in the fullness of the Spirit of God. Otherwise you would not be able to see me as you do.'

Leaning towards me, he whispered in my ear: 'Give thanks to God for his infinite goodness to us. As you have noted, I haven't even crossed myself. It was enough simply to have prayed to God in my thoughts and in my heart while saying: "Lord, make him worthy to see clearly

---

[24] Gregory of Palamas, *Triads*, 38.

with the eyes of his body the descent of your Spirit, with which you bless your servants, when you see fit to appear in the magnificent light of your glory." And as you can see my friend, the Lord immediately granted this prayer of the humble Seraphim.... How thankful we should be to God for this unspeakable gift bestowed on us both. Even the fathers of the desert did not always enjoy such manifestations of God's goodness. For the grace of God – like a mother full of tenderness for her children – has deigned to console your afflicted heart, through the intercession of the Mother of God herself.... Why then, my friend, won't you look at me straight in the face? Look freely, without fear: The Lord is with us.'

Encouraged by these words, I looked and was siezed by a holy fear. Imagine the middle of the sun, dazzling in the radiance of its midday rays, the face of the man who is speaking to you. You see the movements of his lips, the changing expression of his eyes; you hear his voice; you feel the hands that hold you by the shoulders but you see neither his hands nor the body of the person speaking – nothing but the resplendent light which shines and illumines with its brilliance the snow-covered meadow and the snowflakes that never cease to fall....

'What do you feel?' asked Father Seraphim.

'An infinite well-being,' I said.

'But precisely what sort of well-being?'

'I feel,' I responded, 'such tranquillity and peace in my soul. I simply can't find the words to express it.'

'My friend, it is the peace of which the Lord spoke when he said to his disciples: "I give you my peace"; the peace which the world cannot give; "the peace which surpasses all understanding". What else do you feel?'

'An infinite joy in my heart.'

Father Seraphim continued, 'When the Spirit of God descends on someone and envelops that person in the fullness of His presence, the soul overflows with unspeakable joy, for the Holy Spirit fills with joy everything He touches.... If the first-fruits of future joy have already filled your soul with such sweetness, with such happiness, what can we say of the joy of the Heavenly Kingdom that awaits all those who weep on earth? You too my friend have wept during your earthly sojourn but see the joy which the Lord sends you to console you here below.

'This joy, partial and brief, which we feel now, will appear in all its fullness, overwhelming our being with ineffable delights which no one will be able to take from us.'[25]

Vladimir Lossky adds that this tale contains all the doctrines of the Eastern fathers on knowledge. 'The awareness of grace which achieves its highest degree in the vision of Divine Light' is the experience of the Transfiguration and the Resurrection of the Flesh.

The spiritual father hands on not only the traditional doctrine of the resurrection of the flesh, as found in the Creed, but living knowledge acquired in the grace of an encounter, the pure gift of a merciful God. For St Seraphim this experience is not extraordinary. It is 'naturally supernatural' and should be the experience of every Christian. For the Lord said, 'Seek first the Kingdom of God and the rest will be given to you in abundance.' The Kingdom is the Holy Spirit.

St Seraphim adds, 'Some passages of Sacred Scripture seem foreign to us today ... Could one admit the possibility of seeing God in such a concrete mannner? ... We are far from the primitive simplicity of the Christian community. Under the pretext of illumination, we have been plunged into the darkness of ignorance to such an extent that we find inconceivable everything about which the ancients had a very clear notion and could speak about amongst themselves concerning the manifestations of God to humanity as things that were known and not odd in the least.'[26]

In this context to hand on knowledge is to bestow life, to share the light. It is to be a parent in the strict sense of the term, to bring the other to birth in the divine sonship

---

[25] Cited in Vladimir Lossky, *Théologie mystique de l'Eglise d'Orient*, Paris, 1944, pp. 226–227.

[26] Cited in Lossky, pp. 228–229.

that dwells in everyone and in the only-begotten son, to become part of the Trinity.

God alone is Master. God alone is Father. The Gospel says call no one Master, no one Father. All parenthood is a sharing in the Fatherhood of God. This parenthood is but a reflection of the incomprehensible love and inaccessible light of God, who is 'more than being'.

Apophasis, the sense of mystery, leads the spiritual person to humility and to the transfiguration of his entire being in this luminous love.

Chapter Six

The Way of the Pilgrim

The Way of a Pilgrim was published anonymously in 1884 in Kazan. Certain readers perceive behind the apparent simplicity of the tale a true teaching which conveys in a simple manner the tradition of hesychasm. Like the Russian peasant we too are pilgrims on a journey, but on the way towards what awakening? The pilgrim went from church to church, from sermon to sermon, from conference to conference seeking God.

Wise men told him that God was life, the great Breath which animates the universe. All things exist through God, and without God nothing exists. God is not simply this life which will fall victim sooner or later to the law of entropy. No, God is eternal life, uncreated life that does not pass away.

Of course the pilgrim marvelled at all this. 'Perhaps God is eternal life, but how to know God when I am in space and time, how to be rid of fear and anguish, how to be certain that this is not a dream, how to know that the power of the resurrection is already at work in my own depths, how to be certain that I will never die?'

The pilgrim had heard talk amongst the monks about the goal of human life: *theosis* or divinization. He had also heard it said that 'God became human so that we might become God. God bore human flesh so that we might become bearers of the Holy Spirit.'

Once again the pilgrim marvelled at all this. It had been

made clear to him how God, whose essence is unapproachable, allows us to participate in the divine energies and that divinization was a participation in these uncreated energies which the disciples themselves saw streaming from the earthly body of Jesus at the Transfiguration.

The purpose of life is to know this, to participate in divine nature as St Peter said. But how? One must receive the Holy Spirit, for the Holy Spirit makes us like the Son, and in the Son we become one with the Father. Some quoted St Irenaeus to him, 'God the Father fashions us with his two hands, the Son and the Spirit; through them God makes himself known.' The pilgrim believed all this, but nevertheless wanted to see, feel and taste so that this participation might not be mere nostalgia. So he was told, 'You must pray, pray without ceasing, and you will understand.'

The pilgrim said, 'I have heard many excellent sermons on prayer, but they are all instructions on prayer in general. What prayer is, why it's necessary to pray, what the fruits of prayer are. But how does one truly arrive at prayer? No one has told me anything about this. I once heard a sermon on spiritual prayer and perpetual prayer but it didn't have anything to say about how to pray in this way. Listening to sermons never seemed to give me what I wanted. So I stopped going and decided to search for God with the help of a knowledgeable and experienced person who would explain this mystery; for that is what attracted me so persistently.

'Hence, it was no longer a time for lectures and conferences. It was a matter of finding someone knowledgeable and experienced; not just someone with knowledge: such a person would lack the power of being a first-hand witness and transmitting energy. Nor someone who only had experience, who might simply read his experience into mine and who would not have the discernment to counsel me at the particular place on the path I was. It is the blending of knowledge and experience that makes a staretz or master or spiritual father.

There comes a moment in our lives when we can no longer be content with general ideas. We need guidance. The hesychastic tradition, like all the great traditions, insists on person-to-person contact, heart to heart. The mirror in which we can discern the quality (good or bad) of our actions is not some law or rule, but a person. The understanding and love of God comes to us through the look of the staretz, whose knowledge guides us and whose experience reassures us. The pilgrim goes in search of such a guide and finds him in one of the monasteries that flourished in Russia at the end of the nineteenth century.

'To the eyes of the old monk, the government leader, the poor peasant, the student, were all equally in need of spiritual medicine. Some asked him if their son or daughter should marry. Should they accept a certain job? Should they move in order to look for work? ... A peasant woman asked him the best way to feed her turkey.'[1]

The staretz made no long discourses. After he reminded the pilgrim that human wisdom and knowledge are not sufficient for receiving the divine gift (it is rather gentleness and humility which dispose one towards receiving it), he introduced a small practice.

The practice which he suggested is attributed to Symeon the New Theologian in the *Philokalia*. The Greek word *'philokalia'* literally means the 'love of beauty'. Prayer is the art by which a person becomes one with Beauty that is reflected in nature, in bodies and in persons. To pray is to go from the reflection to the source.

The practice that the staretz taught the pilgrim was to sit down alone, be quiet, breathe more slowly, let the mind descend into the heart, invoke the Name while breathing, let go of thoughts, be patient and to repeat this excercise often. Like the words received by Arsenius, this teaching can be interpreted on different levels.

Sit down. It pertains first of all to posture. Be neither rigid

[1]   S. Tchetvenikoff, *L'Ermitage d'Optimo*, French trans. J. Meyendorf, Paris, 1926.

nor limp. You must be at once restful and vigilant like the Bride in the Song of Songs, *I sleep but my heart is awake.*

The right posture is one which allows you to remain the longest time possible without moving or growing tired. The stillness of the body facilitates interior stillness. If the spirit is agitated, then it is even more important to persevere with sitting still.

Interpreted on another level, 'to sit down' means to rediscover your psychological equilibrium, to have an attitude of stability and balance. In French there is the expression *'être dans son assiette'* which well describes the state of a person in harmony with himself.

On a spiritual level, posture could be taken as what St John calls a dwelling place. It is to dwell in God. Abide in God as God abides in us. To dwell in God's love is to have one's foundation, one's seat, one's root in him, always and everywhere.

Be silent. Silence of the lips, silence of the heart, silence of the spirit – three degrees. In silence one approaches the infinite silence of the Divine Presence.

Breathe more slowly. It is not a matter of controlling your breath, nor of measuring it, but of following it, calming it, softening it. Today we know rather a lot about the influence of breathing on the psyche. Paying attention to the breath is a sure means of concentration. One even thinks differently when the breath is calm and deep. When the breath comes to a stop, thought is also, as it were, suspended. One can enjoy the silence. To be attentive to every inhalation and exhalation can take us very far. In the hesychastic tradition awareness of the breath is a true spiritual practice. The breath is *ruah*, the breath of God, the *pneuma*, which we call the Holy Spirit. To breathe deeply and gently is to draw near this Spirit, to feel oneself inhaled and exhaled by God.

Look into your heart. In general the hesychastic tradition is critical of the role of images in prayer. St Gregory of Sinai exhorts his disciples to be on guard against the images that the mind produces. 'Lover of God, be most vigilant. When you are quietly working away and you see a light or fire, within or without, or you see some would-be image of Christ, or of the angels or saints, pay them no heed or you will suffer for it. Nor let your mind fabricate them, for they do nothing but lead the soul astray. The true beginning of prayer is the heart's warmth that consumes the passions and produces in the soul light-heartedness and joy. It grounds the heart in a love that is sure and a sense of fullness that cannot be doubted.'

Simone Weil once said that 'the imagination is used to block the openings through which grace enters.' It is difficult for us to cope with emptiness, the desert which we stuff with mirages.

'The monks are not searching for a particular subjective state, but for real contact, whose effects, such as a warming of the heart, joy, sense of plenitude, are real but fundamentally different from the subjective feelings which correspond to them, because they manifest the real presence of God and not a state of the soul.'[2] Nevertheless some modern monastics use the imagination as a means of making God present to them. A staretz on Mount Athos advised a novice to imagine Christ sitting beside him during his daily prayer. The young novice, who until then had never been able to pray, was now able to pass the entire time of prayer speaking and listening to Jesus. The staretz had asked him not to get caught up in details or to try to picture Jesus' face, but with his imagination simply to enjoy his presence.

In the staretz's teaching to the pilgrim, the imagination was directed towards the heart. Why look outside for the one who is within? For the hesychasts the dwelling place of God, was the heart.

It is the special character of the heart to be on familiar terms with everything, to live not in a world of objects but of presences. The purpose of hesychastic prayer is to have this awakening of the heart, this sensitivity to the divine

___

[2]   J. Meyendorff, *Saint Grégoire Palamas*, Paris, 1959, p. 71.

presence in all things, so that all creation becomes a true epiphany, a manifestation of the inaccessible God.

To have a heart is to live from the centre and to leave behind the fragmented mind with its thoughts that come and go. The heart integrates the personality. Firstly, it brings the intellect down into the heart, an act of integration through which we approach the heart of Christ. Secondly, it raises the vital (and sexual) energies into the heart, transforming their blind rush into the energy of love. The animal dimension of the person is not denied but personalized. Having taught him all this, the staretz asked the pilgrim to invoke the Name of Jesus.

If we repeat this phrase in English, *Lord have mercy*, we run the risk of altering the sound and the meaning. The *Kyrie eleison*, which the monks of Athos repeat, has a different nuance. The ancients attributed great importance to the sound of chant, through which God, so they thought, could pour in divine energy and transform a person. One does not learn to chant from a book. Hence, the traditional importance of initiation.

In addition to the nuance of sound, the translation of the *Kyrie* also presents problems. Doesn't the translation of *Kyrie eleison* as *Lord, have pity*, exact as it may be, alter the full sense?[3] The word 'pity' has a slightly pejorative connotation. *He took pity on me*, one says wanly. We can even reject someone who pities us out of pride or presumption or the inability to love – *I don't want your pity*. But for the ancients the mercy of God is the Holy Spirit, the gift of God's love. *Lord, have mercy* means *You who are, send your Breath, your Spirit upon me and upon everyone and we shall be renewed. Let your Compassion and Goodness be upon me and upon everyone. Do not consider my inability to love you or your world. Make my desire flourish, turn my heart of stone into a heart of flesh.* To this *kyrie eleison*

3 Translator's note: in English we easily distinguish pity from mercy, but in French the word *'pitié'* can mean either pity or mercy. The author's point is that we should understand *'pitié'* not as pity but as mercy.

one normally adds *Jesus* or *Jesus Christ Son of God.*

There can be a certain progression in the repetition of
the phrase. First, one can call upon Jesus as a historical
figure, Jesus of Nazareth. Next, as our Master, whose
teachings, handed on through the centuries, guide and
instruct us even today.

Following this, it is still possible to address Jesus as
Manifestation of God, Incarnation of the Word, the one
who bears the anointing (*christos*) of the Living God, the
beloved son who embodies in the words and gestures of
humanity incomprehensible Love. Jesus is now my interior master, an intimate presence who unceasingly opens
the heart and mind and prevents me from closing myself
within my own narrow judgements. I call out to him as
thirst calls out to the Spring. My invocation digs a well
towards the Living Waters.

Lastly, I can invoke him as Logos, through whom all
things exist and without him, nothing exists (John 1).
Through this invocation I draw near the Light and Life
that illumines everyone (not only Christians). I become
one with the creative intelligence that informs everything.
I reunite with the Love that moves the earth, the stars and
the human heart.

Whether historical master, interior master or Eternal
Master, I make Jesus present by Name and through Him,
with Him and in Him, I enter into the intimacy of the
Source. 'Where I am I wish you also to be.' 'The Father and
I are One.'

The invocation of the Name can be done in a low voice
or in silence. It is surprising the amount of time the
ancients spent in oral prayer (reflecting the Jewish tradition). It is an effective way of attaining true silence of
thought.

Be patient and often repeat this excercise. An artist must be
patient and practise his scales before he can rely on inspi-
ration. Many people would love to become artists
overnight. How many beginners consider themselves
rather advanced in prayer when the Name of Jesus is not

yet even permanently harmonized with the rhythm of their breathing or in their heart! Presumption in the area of prayer is frequent, no doubt, because prayer is not easy to verify. For this reason the ear of the staretz is attuned to recognizing the 'false notes' of ego-inflation. Often, the slightest wound to the ego shows up this pretention for what it is. The staretz also insists on repetition. The calming effect is well known. There comes a time when the act works effortlessly by itself.

The pilgrim was given a progressive training, three thousand invocations a day, followed by six thousand, then twelve thousand. The sheer quantity was shocking, but the staretz reminded the pilgrim that the quality of prayer does not depend on us but on God. All we can offer Him is quantity. It is the time spent on roses that makes them precious.

Prayer must be frequent, for the perfection and cultivation of our prayer does not depend on us. As St Paul says, 'we do not know what to ask for' (Rm 8, 26). Only the frequency has been left in our power as a means of attaining that purity which gives birth to every spiritual good.'[4]

The initial effects of this ceaseless repetition are not the most agreeable. When one allows a light to enter a dark room, the light reveals everything that is hidden or disordered in the room. The first thing light does, after the initial flash, is show us our own shadow. If we remain in the initial flash of brightness, the work will not be accomplished.

'For one week in the solitude of my garden I devoted myself to the practice of interior prayer. At first everything seemed to be going well. Then I began to feel a great heaviness, laziness, boredom, an insufferable sleepiness, and my thoughts enveloped me like mist. Grief-stricken I went to the staretz who understood my state and received me with kindness. He said, "My beloved brother, it is the

---

[4] *The Way of a Pilgrim* (translations are from the author's citation from the French edition, *Récits du pèlerin russe*).

world of darkness which wages this struggle against you, for there is nothing it fears more than prayer of the heart. It tries to harass you and fill you with disgust for prayer. But the enemy cannot act without God's permission and only in the service of necessity. Your humility must undergo trial. It is too soon to attain through excessive enthusiasm even the threshold of the heart; for you would risk falling into spiritual avarice."[5]

* * *

Shatan (Satan) in Hebrew means obstacle. As our desire for union with God in Christ awakens, the obstacle which seeks to impede this union is also aroused. In Judeo-Christian thought, Satan is not the opposite of God nor is he the power of evil and darkness that, as in ancient dualistic schemas, pits itself against the power of goodness and light. He is a creature whose role is to put us to the test, to tempt us in order to strengthen us or simply to show us our level of faith and trust in God.

'Without the demons and snares which insinuate themselves in our path we could not make any progress,' say the fathers of the desert. 'Curiously enough the experience of Being never fails to make the enemy appear. Wherever essential Being manifests itself, the opposing crops up. The enemy is a power which thwarts or destroys the life which God wants. The greater the commitment to the things of God, the more assuredly one will encounter the enemy who is keen to divert one from the right path. It is not a mere pious legend, but one of the givens of experience that cannot be explained logically. As soon as one has received the grace of an experience of Being, something will be coming to upset the state of happiness to which he has been transported by the experience which liberated and now engages him. This is not a matter of some psychological compensation which, through the law of

5   *The Way of a Pilgrim.*

equilibrium, makes depression follow overflowing joy or a state of sadness by an exuberance which the circumstances do not justify.'[6]

The enemy of humanity is our Accuser. When there is no longer an accuser to judge us it will be a sign that we are delivered from Evil and that the one whom Gregory of Nyssa called 'Friend of the human race' will begin his reign in us.

God is not a 'thing' that one possesses, much less something that can be reduced to a commodity. The beginner must beware of spiritual gluttony. The emotion that can stir in the presence of someone whom we love is not as important as this person's presence. The pilgrim learns at this stage of his journey to detach himself from his thoughts and feelings in order not to make idols of them. Anything we can experience of God is but an echo. God's voice remains on the other side of the mountain.

The staretz soon died. After mourning for him the pilgrim discovered the staretz's presence within him. The staretz would appear in his dreams and teach him. In his unconscious the staretz had become a sort of archetype of the wise old man, to be consulted at will.

The Bible and the *Philokalia* remained the pilgrim's sole companions and he always verified his experiences in the mirror of tradition. Gradually the prayer worked itself into the pilgrim. Like Abraham, he walked in God's presence, always returning to God through the invocation. It transformed him and sent him along the path of Fullness.

The Christian is not better than any one else, neither more intelligent nor more loving. The difference is that he walks with Someone and stays in this Presence. It is this Presence, more than any personal effort, which transforms.

It is often said of married couples that as they grow old together they begin to look like each other. And so through living a lifetime of prayer in the presence of God,

---

[6] Attributed of Graf Dürckheim.

one begins to resemble God. You become what you love.

'Look how I go about, ceaselessly repeating the Jesus prayer, which is to me sweeter and more precious than anything in the world. Sometimes I walk fifty-odd miles a day without giving it a thought. I am only aware that I am saying the prayer. When I am beset by some great burden, I recite the prayer with greater attention and soon it is sorted. If hunger becomes too much, I invoke all the more often the name of Jesus and I forget that I'm hungry. If I don't feel well and my back or my legs hurt, I focus on the prayer and I'm no longer aware of the pain.

'Whenever someone insults me, I think of nothing but the gracious Jesus prayer. Very soon the anger or pain subsides, and I forget all about it. I've become a bit odd: nothing really eats away at me; nothing worries me; it just has no hold on me. I'm forever wanting to be in this solitude. By force of habit I have but one need: to recite unceasingly the prayer and when I do it I'm filled with joy. God knows what is taking place in me. Obviously these are only sense impressions or, as the staretz used to put it, the natural effects of an acquired habit. But I still dare not begin studying prayer within the heart.'[7]

Upon reading this tale some will think that prayer is a type of self-hypnosis or psychotropic drug that makes one oblivous to hunger, pain or insult. But none of these effects are to be sought after in themselves. They come and go like everything else. Do not be afraid of becoming a bit odd.

Western mystics, especially St John of the Cross, speak of another fruit of prayer

> Oh living flame of love
> which gently wounds
> the inmost centre of my soul ....

7   *The Way of a Pilgrim.*

Oh sweet burning
delightful wound
light hand, delicate touch
which tastes of life eternal ....[8]

The deep touch of God in the depths of the soul, *o mane blanda! o toque delicado!*

The language of the pilgrim is less poetic, but his experience is no less resonant with that of John of the Cross – after the pain, he speaks of a pleasant warmth and a feeling of consolation and peace. God wounds and heals, humbles and exalts. God plunges in darkness and illumines.

The pilgrim's journey is, above all, interior. He experiences all the emotions a person can have, both positive and negative. Nothing that is human is foreign to him. Still in all this he remains a wayfarer, not stopping in ecstasy, not delighting in his suffering. Such is the path. But more important than these is the understanding of Scripture and the experience of the Transfiguration.

'During this period I also read my Bible and I felt I was beginning to understand it better. I was finding fewer obscure passages. The fathers are correct in saying that the *Philokalia* is the key which unlocks the mysteries buried in Scripture. Under its guidance, I began to understand the hidden meaning of the Word of God; I discovered the meaning of "the interior self in the depths of the heart; true prayer, adoration in the spirit, the Kingdom of Heaven within us, the intercession of the Holy Spirit". I understood the meaning of these words: "You are in me; give me your heart; put on Christ; the betrothal of the Spirit in our hearts; the invocation *Abba, Father*," and many others.[9] And while I prayed in the depths of the heart, everything around me seemed transformed: the trees,

---

[8]   *Living Flame of Love.*
[9]   See Pt. 3.4; Jn 4.23; Lk 17.21; Rm 8.26; Jn 15.4; Pr 23.26; Rm 13.14 and Ga 3.27; Apoc. 22.26; Ro 8.15–16.

grass, birds, earth, air, light – every created thing seemed to proclaim that it bears witness to God's love for humanity. Everything was praying. Everything sang glory be to God! I also understood what the *Philokalia* calls "knowledge of the language of creation", and I saw how it was possible to converse with God's creatures.'[10]

The experience of the Transfiguration alongside the experience of humble love is one of the fundamental characteristics of hesychasm. Following Gregory Palamas, Mount Athos places great emphasis on the realism of this experience which is our participation in uncreated light. Kazantzakis observes that our tendency is to 'humanize God, whereas we should deify the person'.

Christ and the saints, when represented in art, were once entirely surrounded by a halo of light. Then, in Western art, this light became an aura around the face and finally a small crêpe or saucer, as though grace had withdrawn from the human body, no longer manifesting itself in the body but floating like a wisp of cloud above his head.

The pilgrim sees the world as transfigured. He sees that it reveals the 'fire of things'. His eyes have been opened by prayer and have become capable of seeing the glory of YHWH in the body of the world. In Judeo-Christian thought the glory of God evokes an experience of importance, of luminous density. For us glory is nothing but a translation of Roman '*dignitas*', whereas in semitic understanding the glory of a being is its fundamental reality. 'The heavens declare the glory of God' (Ps 19.1). This means that the Uncreated is present in the created. Moses saw the fire in the Burning Bush and in that flame the voice of the Other who said 'I am'. Is this not the same experience as the disciples on the day of the Transfiguration, when their eyes became capable of seeing 'Him as He is'. The apostles, then, contemplate the visible face of the Invisible. They hear the Name of the One who is without

10   *The Way of a Pilgrim.*

a name. They touch, or rather are touched, by the One who dwells in inaccessible light. The Russian pilgrim, for his part, enters into this experience of the Transfiguration which is the goal of hesychast meditation. 'This happiness illumined not only my soul; but the exterior world also appeared to me under a ravishing guise, everything called me to the love and praise of God. Other people, the trees, animals – I felt a bond with them all – and everywhere I found the reflection of the Name of Jesus Christ. At times I felt so light I thought I no longer had a body and floated lightly in the air. Sometimes I entered completely within; I saw clearly my own interior and I admired the remarkable structure of the human body.'[11]

We are in the presence of a spirituality that is not disincarnate, whose problem is not how to escape from the world and the body, but how to allow the Pentecostal flame to descend – how to hasten the Transfiguration of the world.

The way of the pilgrim is not opposed to modern social problems or to the desire for justice. It simply reminds us that social change with no change of heart is in the long run condemned to failure. And the human heart can never change unless it feels, at least once, that it is loved, infinitely loved, and unless it consents to this Love which can deliver it from vanity and greed.

[11] *The Way of a Pilgrim.*

Chapter Seven

The Invocation of the Name in Three Great Spiritual Traditions

To bring the Invocation of the Name in Christianity into dialogue with the Invocation of the Name in the great spiritual traditions of humanity is not to create the religious mixed salad known as syncretism. Rather it is simply to recall the unity of humanity as such. The truth of one tradition ought to be found under its own proper forms and nuances in other traditions. Otherwise it would be an impoverished truth.

To consider these other traditions as necessarily heretical would be against the First Commandment which is to acknowledge the presence of the one Creator in all creation. We must learn to recognize the presence of the Word, the *sperma theou*, the seed of God, in all traditions, which clears a path of light through the obscurity and hardness of the human heart.

Far from diminishing the unique value of the hesychastic way of prayer, the great spiritual traditions of humanity affirm it as one of the great forms through which humanity reaches out to embrace Infinite Reality.

I. The Invocation of the Name in Hinduism

1. *Basic Tenets of Hinduism*

According to Jean Herbert, the fundamental theories of Hinduism are:

(a) The most profound truth is appreciably different from any particular understanding which our sense-perceptions allow us to make, even when these perceptions are interpreted with all the resources of reason.

(b) Beginning from the image which appearances give us, the more we detach from the awareness of multiplicity in order to ascend to the awareness of unity, the more we approach the deep truth.

(c) The visible universe is a manifestiation of the One under the appearance of the many.

(d) The world of polarities, that is, the awareness of the multiplicity in which we live, is an imperfect manifestation of the deep truth. In a certain sense the former participates in the latter according to its nature and serves as a springboard for arriving at this deep truth.

(e) The deep totality must take in not only the totality of that which is, but also that which escapes the categories of existence. It transcends polarities.

(f) The human soul is identical with the totality. By means of appropriate disciplines a person is capable of realizing this identity, and the goal of life is precisely to realize this awareness of profound truth.

(g) Until the soul attains this awareness, it is obliged to reincarnate itself, that is, to pass – or to believe it passes – through a succession of states characterized by birth and death. Hence, it can be said that the purpose of life is to escape this never-ending cycle of reincarnations.

(h) Each incarnation is determined by those which have preceded it and determines to a certain extent those that follow.

(i) Each incarnation, therefore, has characteristics that

particularize it. It differs from others by the possibilities it offers and by the obligations it imposes.

(j) Every soul will finally realize that profound truth called liberation. This can be conceived as union with a personal deity, as unity, as the awareness of non-duality or as a state of awareness which transcends both unity and duality.[1]

It will be necessary to keep these various points in mind when we begin the study of the *Japa-Yoga*, the mental repetition of a sound or the invocation of a name. One cannot overlook the theological and philosophical presuppositions of this method. If one were to remove it from its Hindu context, one would only distort it, and any comparisons with hesychasm regarding posture and method would lead to confusion.

First it is advisable to recall the importance of the word and mantra in Hindu tradition. Then we will consider the meaning that the invocation of a name has in bhakti yoga.

2. *Word, Name and Sound in the Practice of Yoga*

a) The Importance of word and sound in Hindu tradition: *Shabda Yoga*, the Yoga of Mystical sounds.

From the time of the *Vedas*, the sacred and transcendent Word (*vak*) was considered the generative power which sustains and destroys the cosmos. If refers to three things: the way in which the world was created; the cosmic principle that orders and sustains the universe; and mantras as the means of liberation from the world of becoming.

The vehicle of revelation can be either a common language (in which case only the meaning really matters) or a sacred language. In the latter case language has a divine origin capable of being detected in the language itself: its grammar is considered a spiritual discipline, and

[1]   See Jean Herbert, *Spiritualité hindoue*, Paris, 1972.

its sounds haved a symbolic foundation for metaphysical truths. The shape of the letters themselves and their numerical value reveal a sacred mathematics.

The inspired schools of the *Upanishads* have developed an exalted teaching on sounds (*shabda*) and words which proceed from the eternal Word and through which one can enter into communion with it. The eternal Word itself is silent beyond silence.

b) The Mantra

The etymology of *mantra* goes back to the root *man*, meaning to think, and the suffix *tra*, which denotes agency. A mantra literally means 'an instrument thought'. This is not the ordinary, conceptual, discriminating thought that is tied to the empirical world and to subject-object duality, but to a higher form of thought which unifies and liberates awareness.

Sri Aurobindo writes, 'The theory of the mantra is that it is a word born form the hidden depths of our being where it has been nurtured by a deeper awareness and finally emerges either silently or is pronounced out loud precisely for the purpose of creation (the silent word is perhaps considered more powerful than the spoken word). The mantra creates in us new subjective states or modifies our psyche, revealing an awareness as well as faculties that we previously did not know. It also produces them in others. Moreover, the mantra can produce vibations which can in turn produce certain effects such as physical apparitions. The Vedic use of the mantra is nothing but the conscious use of this hidden power of the Word'.[2]

From the Vedic period on, the recitation of passages from the *Veda* is an integral part of most Hindu rites – sacrifices, exorcisms, marriage, initiation. It finds its fullest development in Hindu of Buddhist santrayana tantrism, the way of

---

[2] Sri Aurobindo cited in J. Herbert, *Spiritualité hindoue*, p. 452.

the mantras. These tantric mantras are usually formed by sounds or syllables. 'If one does not know the Syllable which is the abode of all the gods in highest heaven, what would one do with an entire hymn'?[3]

These sounds are 'the resonant and effective bearers of a more fundamental energy and are capable of being used by an adept'.[4] They are rightly called 'seeds' or *bija*. The simplest sounds derive from the very alphabet of Sanskrit, whose every letter is a potent bearer.

c) AUM (OM)

AUM is the primordial sound, the source of every word. It is the basic symbol of the Brahman, the fundamental mantra (*mulamantra*) above all others. It begins religious texts and opens and concludes sacred recitations.

'These three letters, A, U, and M, pronounced together as AUM, can certainly symbolize the sum total of all sounds. The letter A is the least differentiated sound of all; for this reason Krishna says in the *Gîta*: "Amongst the letters of the alphabet, I am 'A' (*Bhagavad Gita*, X, 33)." All articulated sounds are produced in the cavity of the mouth, between the back of the tounge and the lips. "A" is a gutteral sound. "M" is one of the labials. "U" (pronounced "oo" is in "loo") marks a forward movement which begins at the base of the tongue and finishes on the lips. When it is correctly pronounced, this AUM displays the entire phenomenon of sound production, something no other sound can do.'[5]

'The "A" represents an undeveloped state; the "U" is more refined, and the "M" is casual. The "M" relies more and more on the absolute.'[6]

---

[3]   *Rig Veda* I, 164, 39.

[4]   (See A. Padoux, *Recherches sur le symbolisme et l'énergie de la parole dans certains textes tantriques*, Paris, 1975.

[5]   Swami Vivekananda, *Les Yogas pratiques*, p. 179.

[6]   Swami Yatiswarananda cited in J. Herbert, *Spiritualité hindoue*, p. 453.

'The earth is the essence of all beings; water is the essence of the earth; plants are the essence of the waters; humanity is the essence of plants; the word is the essence of humanity; the essence of the word is the vedic verse; the essence of the verse is the melody (*saman*); the essence of melody is the *Udgitha* (the principle part of the melody); AUM is this *Udgîtha*.'[7]

'The goal which all the vedas proclaim and which all the austerities (*tapasaya*) envisage, for the realization of which the *Brahmacharya* is practised, is precisely AUM.'[8]

'AUM is a bow, the "I" (*atman*) is the arrow, and the goal is said to be *Brahman*.'[9]

There is even a Christian interpretation. 'Because AUM is a unique sound composed of three elements it is well-suited to express in an audible symbol the mystery of one Essence in three hypostases: it reverberates like the immanent music of the silent creative deity.'[10]

After being approved by a Catholic religious who accepted the AUM mantra as a manifestation of he Trinity, Ramdas defined AUM in its Hindu context as the unity of natural and supernatural. The mantra is a method of uniting with this divine realm that undergirds all things. 'Ramdas accepts the notion of Trinity: albeit three-fold, there is but One Reality. A Swiss priest and member of a religious order agreed, saying that, though differing in appearance, Father, Son and Holy Spirit are One.

'Now we are going to try to understand the meaning of AUM. It is the combination of three sounds "A", "U", "M".The first sound, "A" symbolizes the creation. 'U' symbolizes preservation, and 'M' destruction. From the primordial silent spirit came forth the sound which in turn brought forth the universe. This sound is a wave rising up to the spirit of God, calm, silent, all-penetrating. It is the

---

[7] *Chandogya Upannishad*, I, 1, 1–2.

[8] *Katha Upanishad*, II, 15.

[9] *Dhyanabindu Upanishad* 15; *Mundaka Upanishad*, II, 2, 4.

[10] J. Monachin in *Ermites du Saccidannanda*, p. 176 and H. le Saux, *Eveil à soi, éveil à Dieu*, Paris, 1971, pp. 124–134.

universe that we see. Such is the explanation offered by Hindu philosophy. What we have before us is not a creation but a manifestation of God and therefore not something comletely different from God. Just as a wave rising out of the womb of the ocean is also the ocean (though revealing only one aspect of it), so in the same way the spirit, who is silent, calm and pure, is God. This vast manifestation is a wave on the divine ocean. From this comes the assertion of the great wisemen of India that the universe itself is Brahman: *servam khalvidam Braham*. Three aspects of a single power appear in this manifestation: one creates; the other preserves; the third destroys. By this practice we return to the silent spirit from which the universal manifestation proceeds, including ourselves. The simplest way, according to the *Upanishads* and the *Vedanta*, consists in constantly modulating the sacred syllable, AUM. It provokes an interior resonance which gives us access to subtle levels of consciousness. When this resonance ceases, our individual existence merges with the supreme Brahman, the unchanging aspect of the divine. This is the meaning of AUM.'[11]

d) Japa

Japa is the repetition of a matra. The mantra is chosen by the teacher and is given to the student during his or her initiation. It is necessary to repeat this mantra as often as possible, up to hundreds of thousands of times a day, often with the aid of a prayer rope. For this to be most effective, centuries of Hindu tradition have developed many tried and tested conditions.

First, one must carefully eliminate the cause of every distraction. Then it is necessary to let the energy, represented by the associations of ideas, dissipate.[12] One must always sit in the same place, in the same position, on the

[11] Ramdas, *Entretiens de Hadeyah*, Paris, 1957, p. 312.
[12] See J. Herbert, *Glossaire du Râja-Yoga et du Hatha-Yoga*, Paris, 1944.

same seat, and facing the same directon. In this way one profits at each sitting from the accumulated benefits of previous sittings. it is advisable to choose a quiet, solitary place, a time when nature itself is peaceful, and above all, to maintain one position (*asana*).

There are a number of these classical meditation postures but they all have certain things in common. One sits on the floor with legs crossed in front, feet close to the body, spinal column, back of neck and head all in a straight line. The position of the hands (*mudras*), eyes (*drishtis*), and certain muscles are also considered important.[13]

The Hindu begins the meditation period with a breathing exercise that purifies the channels of the psychic body (*nadishuddi*). Then begins the japa itself. The japa can be repeated either loudly or softly. Silent repitition is also considered very effective, so long as one maintains attention.

'In reciting the same mantra, the aspirant makes noticeable progress each day without knowing it. In repeating it thousands and thousands of times, the student acquires the required degree of inner concentration and becomes absorbed in the meditation. Kundalini (the essetial energy force) beings to awaken within. When a person's mind is cleansed of every impurity, he or she is completely given over to the japa; the sacred word springs forth spontaneously from the depths of being without the slightest effort. This result is proof that the japa has borne fruit.'[14] The fruit, this liberation from reincarnation, is divine union. 'The soul is nothing but Brahman and is rooted in Brahman.'[15] Brahman is 'the soul's true nature.'[16] The repitition of the mantra in this context is a means of gaining access to the divine, considered as a state of non-duality or a state of jiva (*jîvatva*).

[13] See J. Herbert, *Comment se préparer à la méditation*, Paris, 1943.
[14] *La Vie de Sârada-Devî*, (wife of Ramakrishna), trans M. Sauton, Paris, 1946, p. 184.
[15] *Brihad-arammyaha Upanishad* IV, 4, 6.
[16] *Chândogya Upanishad* VIII, 12, 3.

3.   *The Bhakti Yoga and the Invocation of the Name*

If jnana yoga acknowledges the radical oneness of all
things, bhakti yoga, by contrast, is pre-eminently dualist.
In it, the practitioner desires, not to ground herself in an
awareness of undifferentiated unity, but to rejoice heartily
in the presence of God. It is what Sri Ramakrishna, citing
Ramprasad, meant when he said, 'I don't want to become
the sugar, I want to taste it.'

Which god does the bhakti choose as the object of
adoration? Apparently it matters little, so long as he loves
his god heart and soul. Once the god is chosen, the bhakti
needs only to repeat its name and thus be led to that
ecstasy where 'the Love, the Loving and the Beloved are
but one thing', as Vivekananda says.

'The devout person loses every notion of propriety and
roams the world without ties .... His heart is rooted in
love while he chants the Name of his beloved. An enthusi-
ast (literaly one possessed by God), he might explode in
laughter or begin to weep; he might cry out or sing at the
top of his voice or he could just being to dance.'[17]

Swami Ramdas gives eloquent testimony to this. 'In this
yoga to sing the name of God is the best way to attain it
and it is also the easiest. The *Bhagavad Gita* says: "Amongst
all sacrifices I am the Japa." The sacrifice of the japa
consists in becoming divine through the repetition of his
Name. This should not be done mechanically, and those
who do so will profit little by it. One must wholly participate in it. God and God's Name are not distinct. When you
give it all your love, this name becomes sweeter than
nectar, because as you are chanting it you are giving voice
to the hidden joy within yourself. From the moment you
begin repeating the Name you experience an ineffable
ecstasy. In fact, the Name is not a technique; it is an end in
itself. If you put a sweet in your mouth, you taste immediately the flavour. It is the same when you give yourself
to the divine Name; you experience joy.

[17] *Srimad Bhabavata*, XI, 111.

'Many who repeat this name claim to gain neither profit nor joy. If you truly love God above all else, God's name will immediately delight you. The mere thought of something truly loved from the heart brings joy. A mother, for example, loves her son, and his name is precious to her. Every mother knows this experience. A friend's name alone is enough to bring joy. And so if you give your whole heart to God and repeat God's Name, you will savour its taste.'[18]

'One must repeat the name of God while putting one's whole soul into it, but not with a divided mind which only shows that your love for God is less than total. Some come to Ramdas and complain that they repeat the name with their lips but that their minds wander. Why is it so difficult to keep to the meditation and concentrate the mind on God while repeating God's Name? It is because the love of superficial things is greater than the love of God. Where your love is, there is your mind. If you love God with your whole heart, your mind will be fixed on God. It is just like the miser whose mind is fixed on his treasure.

'The one who aspires to God must think of God as much as, if not more, than the miser who thinks about his hoard. If you love something else more than you love God, your mind will naturally go towards it. That is why the true believer prays: "Lord, grant that I might love you more than the world." If you love like this, your mind will be focused on God, and no thought will distract it.'[19]

'The silent repetition of the Name is esteemed above all. If you repeat it to yourself, your mind will be focused on the name, whereas repeating it out loud will not necessarily stop the roving mind. But if your mind is particularly attuned to sound, then audible repetition is preferable. This is what Ramdas did: the sound steadied his mind and focused it on God, thus uniting it to God. This audible repetition will gradually change itself into

---

[18] Swami Ramdas, *Entrietiens de Hodeyah*, Paris, 1957, p. 32.
[19] Ramdas, *Entretiens*, p. 34.

silent repetition. What is repeated and the one who repeats become one thing. After this the repetition stops just as one stops after arriving at the destination. Ramdas can assure you that in all truth there is no easier exercise than this repetition. It will raise you to the heights and lead to comprehension and knowledge of God. Sri Ramakrishna practised different exercises for twelve years. Finally, however, when someone asked his advice, he recommended only the name of God. It is the fundamental practice.'[20] For Ramakrishna God and God's name are identical (something already noted in the Bhaktirasitasindhu of Rupa Goswami in the seventeenth century).

Even today the followers of Krishna, both in India and in the West, chant

Hare, Rama, Hare Rama,
Rama Rama, Hare, Hare
Hare Krishna, Hara Krishna
Krishna, Krishna, Hare, Hare.

Hindu stories about saints are full of people who attained salvation through even the unintentional recitation of one of the names of God. Ajamila was one such person. He was a great sinner before God, who, at the moment of death, called for his son, Harayana. But the son's name was also one of the names of Vishnu. Vishnu, deeming the utterance to be sufficient,, received into paradise the soul of the deceased.

However, the mere repetition of a divine name is no guarantee that that particular god exists. The deity is chosen in order to sustain the devotion. It is less the object of love that counts in bhakti yoga than the love itself. Love divinizes. Devotion liberates.

A moment will come when the follower will have to abandon the object of his or her devotion in order to realize the 'undifferentiated Absolute' which remains the

[20] Ramdas, *Entretiens*, p. 33.

goal, but which our weakness has had to represent itself in a personal way. Swami Vivekananda said, 'In this world there are two types of people who reject the notion of a personal God. One is the rogue incapable of conceiving of such a thing and the other is the rare individual who has elevated herself beyond this notion to the undifferentiated Absolute.

II. The Invocation of God's Name in Islam: The Dhikr

The Dhikr is the Sufi invocation of the name of God, a spontaneous vocal prayer indefinitely repeated. A word, a formula, a verse, a litany of divine names taken from the Koran, are consciously repeated. The pace can vary from slow to rapid enough to leave one gasping for breath. Nervous tension turns into spiritual attention. The soul no longer centres upon the sound of the word but on the meaning, which transports the person to the heart of the desired Object. The prayer directs towards God thoughts, desires, feelings, sensations, images, the entire mental festival in which the soul risks dissipating itself. The practice of dhikr is based not only on psychological observation, but also on the precept from the Koran, 'Recite what is revealed to you from the Book and complete the prayer; in truth the prayer prevents you from giving yourself over to dispersion and to commiting abominations. And certainly it helps you remember that God is great.'[21]

It is precisely this remembrance of God that sharpens the Sufi's awareness of the only existing Reality, *La ilaha illa allah*, only God is God. The dhikr focuses the mind on this fundamental truth, and bit by bit the mind slips from the invocation, which is far from monotonous or anaesthetizing, into silent contemplation.

The Sufi uses beads to count the number of invocations and litanies. This prayer-rope has ninety-nine beads that

[21] Koran XXIX, 45.

correspond to the ninety-nine attributes of God. One holds each bead, one after the other, while pronouncing the sacred words, rather like a rosary. During the common exercises, which are often accompanied by music, the Sufi holds the prayer-rope in his hands.

The experience can end in escstasy, but this should never be sought in itself. Parapsychological states are not always signs of divine presence. Mystical union is not the fruit of a mechanical process. Love is not conquered by mere technique. Indeed, the dhikr can be an obstacle to the vision of God, if it remains the focus of awareness.

The practice of dhikr can be adapted in different ways according to place and occasion. The goal is to renounce the world in order to lead an ascetic life, breaking ties and emptying the heart of its worldly occupations. Although the Sufi aims to lose himself in God, the aim is never to become one with God.

All Sufis acknowledge the teaching of the illustrious theologian, Al-Ghazzali (1058–1111). The highest achievement of the dhikr is not in the power of the dhikr. It depends on Allah. The Sufi can and must practice this exercise. 'It is in the Sufi's power to arrive at the limit and to make it last while fighting off temptations. However, it is not in the Sufi's power to attract the Mercy of God the Most High. But by what he does, the Sufi gradually begins to receive the breaths of divine Mercy and he can do nothing but await what the Most High reveals of the divine Mercy, just as God did to the Prophets and saints .... Ultimately this path, as far as you are concerned, leads to complete purity, purification and clarity and then to being ready to wait.'

III. The Invocation of the Name in Buddhism

1.   *Pure Land Buddhism and the Vow of the Buddha*

It was in Japan, in the Kamakura period, that the monk, Honen, founded a new Buddhist sect, called Pure Land, dedicated to the practice of Nembutsu (the invocation of the name of Buddha).

Pure Landers belived that, however laborious human effort might be, the good works accomplished under one's own steam are not enough to lead to the fullness of illumination in this life. For this reason the Buddha taught that the only possible way for ordinary people to achieve such illumination was to trust in the Buddha's compassion. He desired to save all sentient beings, bar none.

According to the great Sukhavati-vyuka Sutra, the Buddha made forty-eight special vows, the most important of which was the eighteenth: 'When I arrive at the threshold of Buddhahood, if there are beings with sincere hearts in ten directions of the compass, who are happy and desire to be re-born in my land, but who, while invoking my Name only ten times are not reborn there, I should prefer not to cross the threshold of highest illumination.'

That is, if someone has faith in the Buddha and pronounced his Name, he will without fail be re-born in his Pure Land and will be able to cross the threshold of highest illumination. No other discipline is required to obtain this re-birth in Nirvana. Honen called this vow 'the vow of re-birth (in the Pure Land) by means of Nembutsu', for it is only by Nembutsu that ordinary people can achieve illumination. 'To say the Nembutsu and to become Buddha, is the whole of Buddhism.'

2.   *The Practice of Nembutsu*

In Pure Land the Buddha is known as Amida, *Namu Amida Butsu*. The words mean: *Namu* – I take refuge in, I take joy in, I venerate. *Amida* – infinite light (Amitabha) and eternal life (Amitayus), eternal wisdom, great compasion. *Butsu* – the Buddha. According to the interpretation of the Chinese Master Zendo, he is called infinite because all who think on him are embraced and never again abandoned.

Ippen Shonin (1229–1289) says, 'You ask me about the proper mental attitude to have towards Nembutsu. The only thing required is to say "Namu Amdia Butsu"; there is no other instruction that I could possibly give you. In saying "Namu Amida Butsu" you will discover your essential peace.'

'One day someone asked Kuya Shonin (+972): "How should one say the Nembutsu?" He simply said, "Let go." There were no other words. This response has been preserved in Saigya's anthology of poetry, and in my view it is a gem. "Let go." It is all that is required of the one who is faithful to Nembutsu. Let such a one also abandon knowing, wisdom and ignorance as well as every notion of good and evil, rich and poor, noble and serf, heaven and hell, and all types of satori that the various schools of Buddhism cultivate and teach. Rejecting all the ideas and desires, which only cause confusion, abandon yourself entirely to saying "Namu Amida Butsu!"

'Since this is in perfect accord with the great Vow of Amida, recite the Nembutsu with a mind ever more unified.

'The moment will come when you will understand that while reciting 'Namu Amida Butsu" there is neither Buddha nor I nor any sort of reasoning process one has to go through.

'Whatever the conditions in which you find yourself, whether they be good or bad, the Land of Purity is always open to you, for here there is nothing to look for and nothing to avoid. Every living being, the mountains and rivers, the grass and the trees, the flowing breeze and the rolling waves say in one voice the Nembutsu.

'My only wish is that as you rediscover your simplicity and original innocence you say the Nembutsu: "Namu Amida Butsu".'[22]

'The one who takes refuge in the Buddha, does not take refuge in a being with a head and arms, etc., a being born of a mother and father, but in the inconceivable qualities by which one merits to be called Buddha; in other words in the essential body.'[23] This essential body, Buddhahood, is the true nature of everyone.

---

[22] Cited in J. Eracle, *La Doctrine bouddhique de la Terre Pure*, Dervy Livres, 1973, pp. 69–70

[23] Dharmakaya.

Chapter Eight

The Invocation of the Name
in Christianity

I. Theological Presuppositions Concerning Prayer
of the Heart

1. *Historical Foundations*

In 313, the Edict of Milan made Christianity legal throughout the Roman Empire, and the first great age of martyrs
was over. However, a strong reaction, anticipated by the
Egyptian hermits, against the conformism of Constantine
ensued. A baptism of asceticism succeeded the martyr's
baptism of blood. No longer did the Christian go meekly
and humbly to the arena to do battle with the forces of
evil, but rather to the desert. From then on the Christian's
mission was, as St Anthony said, 'to loosen the stronghold
of the demons' and to introduce of the Kingdom of God in
peace and love. These men and women in the desert are
the ancestors of the hesychasts, who, from the fourth
century to the present day, form an unbroken tradition.

The word *hesychasm* was a well-established technical
term by the seventh century. John Climacus dedicates one
chapter to hesychasm in his treatise, *The Ladder of Divine
Ascent*. In the fifth century it is represented by such figures

as Nilus of Ancyra (or the Sinaite), St Diadochus of Photiki and St John the Hesychast, whose life is recounted by Cyril of Scythopolis.[1]

What is hesychasm? It is a spirituality founded upon the necessity of *hesychia:* tranquillity, silence, peace of mind. As Irénée Hausherr has said, 'there are many types of peace, from the absence of war to the suspension of mental faculties in mystical repose, from inertia and idleness to the silence of everything and everyone, the calming of the spirit and the heart. There are as many forms of peace as there are beings susceptible to agitation, and all of them come under the concept of hesychia. Just as there is a hesychia of the city, there is an inner hesychia which results from well ordered faculties. According to Plato, the nobility are forever disposed to living a peaceful life.

In Christianity hesychia is a means to union with God. It is not the goal itself as *apatheia* (dispassion) is amongst the Stoics or *ataraxia* (freedom from passion) amongst the Epicurians.

Christian hesychia means above all a life of solitude, silence and perpetual prayer, of men and women who have withdrawn into the desert to taste the peace which the world cannot give. In such an environment the various methods of prayer developed, particularly the prayer of the heart (or the Jesus Prayer), which even today is considered the very soul of the Christian East.

This spiritual tradition has its origins in the monasteries of sixth-century Sinai and on Mount Athos, especially in the fourteenth century with Gregory of Palamas.

In the nineteenth century, the prayer of the heart spread beyond the Athonite monasteries as a result of the *Philokalia*, published in 1782 by a Greek monk, Nikodemus of the Holy Mountain, and published a little later in Russian by Velitchkovsky. Seraphim of Sarov, John of Kronstadt, the holy men of Optino, Theophane the Recluse

---

[1] 'Acta Sanctorum', III, in A.J. Festugière *Les Moines d'Orient*, III, 3 (Paris, 1963), pp. 13–14.

and Ignace Brianchaninov passed on the practice of this prayer to the people. At the end of the nineteenth century, *The Way of a Pilgrim* and the Orthodox churches overseas began to spread its fame to the West.

From the desert fathers to the Russian pilgrim, passing by way of Sinai and Mount Athos, there are slight variations in the method or wording of the invocation, but the spirit is the same.

At risk of being dishonest one cannot remove a technique from its ecclesial and monastic context. Knowledge of the milieu wherein the prayer is practised allows one to discern the theological presuppositions. For example one need not oppose prayer of the heart and liturgical prayer. They are two different ways to the same end: union with the God of Jesus Christ.

So before beginning with questions of technique, it would be well to recall the importance of the Name in Judaeo-Christian tradition and to analyse the theological content of the invocation, *Lord Jesus Christ, Son of God, have mercy on me a sinner.*

2. The Importance of the Name in Judaeo-Christian Thought

In semitic thought a name designates in a general way the hidden nature of something, a sort of active presence. To know someone by name is to know his or her depths and to hold power over them. Hence, to know the name of God is to have power.

If the invocation of the divine name was the most solemn and important act of all ancient religions, it was also the most ambiguous. It seems that in such mentalities, the step from a religious attitude to a magical attitude is very small indeed and is often crossed.

In law, a name designates a relationship of ownership or superiority and guarantees a contract or an oath. 'Moses then said to God, "Look, if I go to the Israelites and say to them, 'The God of your ancestors has sent me to you' and they say to me, 'What is his name?' What am I to tell them?" God said to Moses, "I am he who is." And he said, "This is what you are to say to the Israelites, 'I am has sent me to you.'" God further said to Moses, "You are to tell the Israelites, 'Yahweh, the God of your ancestors, the God of Abraham, the God of Isaac and the God of Jacob, has sent me to you.' This is my name for all time, and thus I am to be invoked for all generations to come'" (Ex 3.13–15).

For Moses, God's name is 'He is' because in the Burning Bush God allowed Moses to experience Being itself. 'This he showed you, so that you might know that Yahweh is the true God and that there is no other.... Hence, grasp this today and meditate on it carefully: Yahweh is the true God, in heaven above as on earth beneath, he and no other' (Dt 4.35, 39).

The name of YHWH thus becomes responsible for all the great events of God in Israel, both in history and in nature: the deliverance of his people; conquests of foreign invaders; the creation and ordinance of the Cosmos.

While revealing his name God also gives it to the people so that eventually they might possess him. Israel has the power to pronounce this name and its mission will be to glorify and sanctify it in the midst of other nations. 'When the Israelites do the will of God, his name is exalted throughout the world (e.g. Joshua and Rahab); but when they do not do God's will, God's name is in a sense profaned throughout the world,' said Rabbi Eleazar (*c*. AD 200).

To belong to this holy people is to bear the name of YHWH (Deuteronomy 28.9–10; Jeremiah 15.16). Although it is not a fetish, it cannot be doubted that the Name was practically considered an instrument, a vessel of divine presence in the heart and mouth of the believer.

The glorification of the Name of God eventually becomes the only thing towards which the holy ones of YHWH aspire. Their prayers are unified by a single purpose, that all creatures might know God. This becomes a confession of faith, sung in the liturgy and acclaimed in songs of praise.

3. *The Name of YHWH, 'Figure of Christ'*

The name of YHWH fufilled two roles for the faith of Israel: revelation of God's saving plan and a progressive knowledge of God acquired through his saving acts. The person of Christ is the manifest realization of these two roles. On the one hand, Christ reveals the mystery and plan of God. On the other hand he unifies in himself all previous Revelation. He takes on his role (Matthew 23.27), he gives the definitive meaning to all the prophecies and he is the truth of all God's saving acts in the Old Testament.

The name of YHWH reveals God in person and at the same time protects his transcendence. *I am who I am*. St John says of Christ, 'Anyone who has seen me has seen the Father' (Jn 14.9), but without denying that 'No one has seen the Father' (Jn 6.46). In the relationship of the name to YHWH and in Christ to the Father there is a remarkable analogy, from the point of view of revelation.

How could one not ascribe unique value to those passages from St John (8.24, 28, 58; 13.19) where Jesus identifies himself with the sacred Name of YHWH – I am. Jesus did not say that his name was 'I am' but that he himself was 'I am'.

One can also connect the characteristics of the theophany at Sinai (the Cloud and the voice which showed the meaning of the divine name) with the characteristics of the theophany seen in the Transfiguration (the cloud – the Voice which confirmed the authority of the mission of the Son – Matthew 17.5), a connection which the presence of Moses makes still more meaningful.

Henceforward the new people of God will no longer pray in the name of YHWH but in the name of Jesus. 'The Father will give you anything you ask him in my name' (Jn 15.16). 'Since he did not spare his own Son, but gave him up for the sake of all of us, then can we not expect that with him he will freely give us all his gifts?' (Rm 8.32).

St Peter declared: 'For all the names in the world given to men, this is the only one by which we can be saved'

(Ac 4.12). Never was the identification clearer between the name and the person it represented and nowhere does one see better how Christ substitutes himself for the name of YHWH, the sole refuge of salvation for the Jew.

Thinking of 'his hour', the Passion which preceded his Glorification, Jesus said, 'Father, glorify your name' (Jn 12.28) and 'Father ... glorify your Son' (Jn 17.1). This sacred and fundamental element of Judaism, which was the Name of YHWH, is fulfilled in the Incarnation of the Son of God. Christ received from God 'the name which is above all other names' (Ph 2.9). This name is *Kyrios* (= YHWH) and expresses the transcendent nature of God. From now on it assumes the place of a divine name in faith and worship.

Calling on the Name of Jesus, the disciples heal the sick (Acts 3.6; 9.34), expel demons (Mark 9.38; 16.17; Luke 10.17; Acts 16.18–19) and perform miracles (Matthew 7.22; Acts 4.30).

The early Christians identified themselves as those who call on the Name of the Lord (Acts 9.14, 21; 1 Corinthians 1, 2; 2 Timothy 2.22). The hesychasts form part of this tradition. To repeat to oneself the Name of Jesus is to walk in his presence and be delivered from every evil. 'What can we say about this sacred prayer, the invocation of the Saviour: "Lord, Jesus Christ, Son of God, have mercy on me"? It is a prayer, a vow, a profession of faith which confers upon us the Holy Spirit and the divine gifts, which purify the heart and expel demons. It is the presence of Jesus in us, a source of spiritual meditation. It is the remission of sins, the healing of body and soul, the ray of divine illumination; it is a fountain of divine mercy which showers forth upon the humble the manifestation of and initiation into the mysteries of God. It is our only salvation, for it contains in itself the Name of God, the only name upon which we can call, the Name of Jesus Christ, the Son of God, "for of all the names in the world given to men, this is the only one by which we can be saved" (Ac 4.12).

'That is why every believer should confess this name,

both to proclaim our faith and to witness to our love of the Lord Jesus Christ, from whom nothing can separate us; and also because of the grace given to us through his name, because of the remission of sins, of healing, sanctification, illumination and above all the salvation which it brings us. Scripture says "these are recorded so that you may believe that Jesus is the Christ, the Son of God." Believe! This is the faith. The Gospel adds: "and that believing this you may have life through his name" (Jn 20.31). Here one finds salvation and life.'[2]

This power of the Name has recently been taken up by Bulgakov. 'The power of this prayer does not reside in its content which is very straightforward, but in the gentle name of Jesus. The ascetics attest that this name captures the power and presence of God. God is not simply invoked by this name but is already present in the invocation. One can certainly affirm it as the entire name of God, but it is necessary to say it above all of the divine-human name of Jesus which is the proper name of God and humanity. Succinct as it is, the name of Jesus present in the human heart bestows on this heart the power of deification which the redeemer has given us.'[3]

Bulgakov does not say, as the Russian pilgrim said, that 'the Name of Jesus contains in itself a salvific power which exists and acts in itself.' Rather it opens the way to the worship of a name. In fact, at the end of the nineteenth century the Jesus Prayer became an anchor of devotion to the very name *Jesus*. The Name of Jesus, was seen to be fundamentally identical to his person and inseparable from his essence. Therefore, it was intrinsically efficacious when invoked and led infallibly to contemplation. This doctrine was spread by two Athonite monks, Hilarion and Anthony Bulatovitch. The teaching was eventually condemned both by the Patriarch

2   Symeon of Thessalonica, quoted in Chariton, *L'Art de la prière*, Bellefontaine, 1976, p. 118.
3   Bulgakov, *L'Orthodoxie*, Paris, 1932, p. 200.

Germain V of Constantinople and by the Holy Synod of Russia.

For the Christian tradition, the Name is not a fetish. It finds its only efficacy in the faith of the one who pronounces it. St Basil the Great thus begins his *Long Rules*, 'If someone says that it is written that whoever invokes the Lord will be saved (Acts 2.21) and if someone wants to infer from this that the mere invocation of the Name of God is enough for Christians to be saved, one need only listen to what the Apostle says, *How then are they to call on him if they have not come to believe in him?* (Romans 10.14). *And if you still do not believe, listen to what Our Lord says: It is not anyone who says to me* Lord, Lord *who will enter the kingdom of Heaven, but the person who does the will of my Father in heaven*' (Matthew 7.21).

John of Kronstadt says that the power of the name is inseparable from the fervour which comes from the heart of the one who pronounces it. 'A heart whose faith is not firmly established can only imagine that the cross and the name of Jesus act miraculously by themselves and not through Christ. The cross and the name of Jesus do not work miracles if I cannot see the Lord Jesus with the eyes of my heart or my faith and if I do not believe with my whole heart what he has accomplished for my salvation. . . . Never pronounce the name frivolously.'[4]

It is the christological content of the prayer that counts above all. 'The Jesus Prayer in its complete formulation refutes all heresies. The word "Lord" manifests the divine nature of Christ and refutes the heresy that says he is only human and not God. The "Jesus", on the other hand, manifests the human nature of Christ and refutes the heresy that says Jesus was only God and only appeared to be human. The word "Christ" manifests the two natures, divine and human, in one person and one hypostasis and refutes the heresy that says Christ has two separate hypostases. The phrase "Son of God" shows that in Christ

---

[4] John of Kronstadt, *Ma vie en Christ* (in Russian), Moscow, 1894.

the divine nature is not confused, even after the union it achieves with the human nature; and the human nature is likewise unmixed and refutes the heresy of those who say that the divine and human natures underwent confusion and are mixed with each other.'[5]

One could never comment enough on the christological character of the prayer of the heart. This prayer emphasizes both the earthly life of the incarnate Lord Jesus Christ and the divine Son of God. However, while it is christological, the Jesus Prayer is not a meditation on the individual events of the life of Christ. Here, as in other forms of prayer, the use of mental images and intellectual concepts is strongly discouraged.

4. Beseeching Mercy, the essential character of the prayer of the heart and its theological presuppositions

Beyond the name itself, the other parts of the prayer also have a biblical foundation. One calls to mind two characteristic prayers in the Gospels, that of the man born blind, 'Jesus, Son of David, have pity on me,' (Lk 18.38) and that of the publican, 'God, be merciful to me, a sinner' (Lk 18.13). For Christians, 'son of David' quite naturally becomes 'Son of God'.

The prayer of the heart, which takes up these words of the man born blind and the publican, is above all a prayer of beseeching and of repentance. The prayer of the hesychast, like the prayer of every Christian, is the prayer of a person who recognizes himself or herself as a sinner. 'The beginning of salvation is to accuse oneself.' No sentence will be more often repeated by all the masters of monastic spirituality: Anthony, Arsenius, Ammoes, Poemen, Theodore of Pherme, etc.

Still more numerous are the examples which put this doctrine into practice. In the monastic tradition everything

---

[5]   A monk cited by I. Haussherr, *Noms du Christ et voies d'oraison*, Rome, 1960, p. 279.

is tied to this: to weep for one's sins is the *sine qua non* of the novice and even more so a sign of progress on the way of perfection. If one takes this path of salvation by admitting one's sinfulness, one will progress by the same means. 'The closer one comes to God, the more one sees oneself as a sinner. When the prophet Isaiah saw God he immediately called himself wretched and impure,' said Abba Matoes.

The monks preferred the way of *penthos* or repentance over every other because they considered it more effective and a better guarantee against illusion. For them prayer was simply to stretch out one's hands towards God in order to receive.

According to Irenaeus of Lyons, a human being is essentially a capacity to receive God's goodness. One accepts this humble and magnificent role and gives thanks for it: a needy creature before God who is infinitely rich and without need.

The monks thanked God but were discrete in their supplication, especially in their liturgy. The object of the supplication is eternal salvation and everything that is directly related to it. Other issues that have no immediate connection with salvation are also welcomed by the Lord who often responds by miracles. But this working of wonders has a negligible role in the lives of the great ascetics. They have better things to ask for, such as God's grace, benevolence, charity and salvation. Their frequent invocations and petitions give nothing but a momentary expression to something which is always with them, their poverty before God.

The treatise of St Nilus expresses this clearly. 'Pray first to receive the gift of tears, so that compunction might soften the inherent hardness of your heart and, while you confess your sins to the Lord, pray to obtain pardon.' We are quite far from the attitude of someone who invokes the Name simply to arouse in himself the energies of divine life. It is a question of admitting one is a sinner and in need of the Lord's mercy to rediscover one's original beauty.

Underlying this attitude an entire theology of creation and redemption in Jesus Christ is presupposed.

In order to have the essence of the prayer of the heart, one needs the name of the Saviour that contains an act of faith in his messiahship, in other words, an act of adoration, a request for mercy, and an act of penance. 'Have mercy on me' also means 'give me your Holy Spirit that I may live with the Son, who was with the Father from the beginning, an eternal Trinity.'

5. The Goal of Prayer of the Heart

From John Cassian to *The Way of a Pilgrim*, the goal is union with God through unceasing prayer.

It is well to place this search for perpetual prayer in its biblical context, for it is fundamentally a question of following the teachings of Jesus, '... pray continually and never lose heart' (Lk 18.1). 'Stay awake, praying at all times' (Lk 21.36). These words echo St Paul who says 'Pray constantly' (1 Th 5.17). 'In all your prayer and entreaty keep praying in the Spirit on every possible occasion' (Ep 6.18).

These are the exhortations which started the pilgrim on his way. 'I am by the grace of God a Christian and by my actions a great sinner.... On the twenty-fourth Sunday after Pentecost I found myself at church praying while Mass was going on. The First Letter of Paul to the Thessalonians was being read: "Pray constantly." This verse entrenched itself in my memory, and I began to reflect how it was possible to pray without ceasing, since humans are obliged to be concerned with many things.

'"What must I do?" I said to myself. "Where will I find someone who can explain this to me? I'm going to visit every church in which there is a renowned preacher; perhaps there I will hear something which will clarify this matter for me." And that's what I did. I heard many excellent sermons on prayer: on what prayer is, on how it is necessary for us to pray, and on the fruits of prayer. But no one ever said how to pray without ceasing. I heard one sermon on continuous prayer, but it said nothing about the means by which one might attain it.'[6]

Many others had asked themselves this question fifteen centuries earlier. The monks did not go into the desert to be malcontents and grasp at straws nor to sacrifice themselves for the Glory of God, but to devote all their inner resources to the love and service of God.

The goal of the monk or nun and the perfection of the heart consists in an uninterrupted perseverence in prayer. In as much as it is given to human frailty, he or she strives for unstirring tranquillity of soul and perpetual purity. And such is the reason we undertake manual labour and seek every opportunity for contrition of heart.

The kingdom of heaven, the infinitely rich reality that we call love and which is not merely a likeness but a participation in Divine Love – it is the Christian realization of humanity's age-old dream, 'to become like God in the measure possible'.[7]

In this way we shall perfectly realize the prayer that our Saviour made to the Father on behalf of his disciples, 'that the love with which you loved me may be in them, and so that I may be in them' (Jn 17.26). The utter delight with which God first loved us will come into our hearts by the fulfilment of this prayer, which our faith tells us will not be in vain. God will be our entire love and desire, our efforts, our thoughts, our life, our speech and breath. The unity of the Father and the Son will be communicated to us in feeling and in spirit. We will be so attached to God that our breath, our minds, and every word we utter will be nothing but God.

'At last it will be accomplished in us what our Saviour desired for us when he prayed ... "That they may be one as we are one. With me in them and you in me, may they be so perfected in unity..." (Jn 17.22–23). "Father, I want those

---

6   *The Way of a Pilgrim.*
7   Plato, *Theaetetus*, 176.

you have given me to be with me where I am" (Jn 24).

'This should be the goal of the monk. All his efforts should be directed to this: to be worthy of possessing in this life an image of future happiness and to have a foretaste in this body of the life and glory of heaven. This is, I say, the goal of all perfection: that the soul be as far away as possible from the weight of the flesh, that it ascend each day towards the things of the spirit, until all its life, every movement of its heart becomes a single uninterrupted prayer.'[8]

The goal of the prayer of the heart is to experience the grace that dwells within us from the moment of baptism. The monks of the Christian East insist especially upon this experience of light and tie it to the experience of the disciples on Mount Tabor.

'We do not speak about what we do not know,' says Symeon the New Theologian, 'rather we give witness to something that is known by experience. For the light already shines in the darkness, by night and by day, in our hearts and in our minds. This light that does not wane illumines us unfailingly and incessantly and is never eclipsed. It speaks; it acts; it lives; it gives life, and it transforms in light what it illumines. God is light and those whom God deems worthy of seeing him see him as light. Those who have received God receive God as light.'[9]

This light is the visible aspect of divinity. It is not of an intellectual order, as illumination of the intellect is sometimes taken in its allegorical and abstract sense. Nor is it something on the level of the senses. This light fills both the intelligence and the senses and reveals itself to the whole person, not simply to a particular faculty. But since it is also a mystical gift, this divine light goes beyond both the senses and the intelligence.

'The Athonite monks say that the light of the mind is different from the light perceived by the senses. Sensible light shows us sensible objects, while intellectual light

8   Cassian, *Conference*, 10, 7.
9   *Homily*, 79, 2, 318–319.

serves to reveal the truth that is in our thoughts. Therefore, the eyes and the mind do not perceive one and the
same light, rather each of the two faculties acts according
to its nature and limits. However, when those who are
worthy receive the grace and the spiritual and supernatural power, they perceive by their senses as well as by
their intelligence what is beyond the senses and the intellect.... How this is so is known only by God and by those
who have had the experience of this grace.'[10]

The light which the Apostles saw on Mount Tabor is
proper to God by nature. Before Christ it was terrifying
and unbearable to creatures. That is why, according to
Symeon the New Theologian, Paul, who had not yet come
to believe in Christ, was blinded and thrown to the ground
by the appearance of divine light while on his way to
Damascus. But Mary Magdalen, who believed, could see,
according to Gregory Palamas, the light of the Resurrection which filled the tomb and illumined everything,
inspite of the darkness. Moreover, this light made her
capable of seeing the angels and conversing with them.

At the time of the Incarnation, divine light concentrated
itself, as it were, in Christ, the God-Man in whom dwelt
the fullness of divinity. Therefore Christ always shone
with divine light during his early life, a light which
remained invisible to most. The Transfiguration was not
something bound by space and time. The change was not
in Christ but in his Apostles, who momentarily received
the capacity to see their Master as he was, resplendent
with the eternal light of divinity.

'The light of the Transfiguration of the Lord had no
beginning or end. It remained uncircumscribed (by space
and time) and imperceptible to the senses even though it
was contemplated by the physical eyes.... But by a transformation of their senses the disciples of the Lord passed
from the flesh to the Spirit.'[11]

[10] Gregory Palamas, PG 150, 1233 D.
[11] Palamas, Sermon 20.

To pray without ceasing, to invoke the name of the one who is our Salvation and our Light and to participate in the divine nature, is quite simply the goal of prayer of the heart in Christianity. It presupposes not only an entire theology of the nature of God but also an anthropology, a way of seeing humanity as capable of receiving Grace and being transformed by it.

II. Anthropological Presuppositions of Prayer of the Heart

1. Introduction

Gregory of Palamas says that 'the one who participates in the divine energy becomes himself light in a certain sense. He is united to the light and, by means of this light, he sees in full awareness all that remains hidden to those who do not have this grace. It goes beyond not only the physical senses but also everything that can be known by the intelligence, ... for the pure of heart see God, ... who, being light, dwells amongst them and reveals Himself to those who love Him.'[12]

The body poses no obstacle to mystical experience. 'We do not apply the term human separately to the body or to the soul but to both at the same time, for the whole person was created in God's image.'[13]

The body must become 'a spiritual body', to use St Paul's expression. The blessed will see God face to face in the fullness of their created natures. 'If the body must take part with the soul in the ineffable riches of the age to come, it must in so far as possible also participate in them from this moment on, ... for the body too experiences God when the passionate forces of the soul find themselves not put to death but transformed and sanctified.'[14]

---

[12] Palamas, *Homily on the Presentation of the Blessed Virgin in the Temple.*
[13] Palamas, *Dialogues on the Soul and the Body*, PG 150, 1361 C.
[14] I. Haussher, 'The Way of Hesychastic Prayer', *Orientalia Christiana Periodica* 36 (1927) 164.

The methods used by the hesychasts have no purpose other than to prepare the person for this transformation of one's entire being in divine light. According to the monks, these methods have no efficacy in themselves. Their success, as we have seen, is in the luminous and salvific presence of the one whose Name we invoke. Before beginning these psycho-physical practices employed by the hesychasts, one should recall that these exercises can be dangerous and should only be used with the greatest discretion, preferably under the guidance of an experienced teacher.

As Nicephorus the Solitary said, 'The good effects of the exercise come for the most part, if not entirely, from the teacher. It would be quite rare indeed for someone to receive from God by sheer application and fervent faith without going through the teacher. But the exception does not make the rule. Therefore it is important to seek out a reliable guide. The guide's teachings show us how we have strayed from the path, our excess as regards attention. The guide's personal experience of trials illumines the way for us and shows us beyond all doubt the spiritual path which we may now embark upon without difficulty. If you have no master, find one at all costs. If you find none, call upon God with a contrite spirit and with tears. Beseech God in nakedness of spirit and do as I tell you.'

'In the absence of a staretz it is generally better to practise only the prayer itself, without bothering with the physical practices, which, Bishop Brianchaninov says, "One should not practise unless they start on their own. . . . One can rightly replace them with a peaceful repitition of the prayer. One ought to make a brief pause between each invocation. The breath should be calm and peaceful, and the mind should concentrate on the words of the prayer."

'Seated in the corner of a quiet cell, do as I tell you. Close the door and raise your mind above every concern. Then, resting your beard upon your chest and turning your eyes and your entire concentration towards the middle of the stomach, the navel in other words, slow down your breath as it passes through your nose. Search your entrails in order to find your soul. At first you will find a darkness and an oppressive heaviness. But if you persevere in this practice night and day, you will discover unending happiness. As soon as the spirit finds the place of the heart, it suddenly perceives what it had never known. For it sees the air at the centre of the heart and it sees itself completely luminous and full of discernment. Henceforth, as soon as there is the slightest thought, before it has a chance to take form, it pursues it and anni- hilates it. From this moment the spirit, in its fight against the demons, awakens anger which is according to its nature and defeats these spiritual enemies. The rest you will learn with the help of God while exercising vigilance over the mind and keeping Jesus in your heart. For, as it is said, sit in your cell, and your cell will teach you every- thing.'[15]

2. Art of Still Prayer

a) Sitting in solitude: the posture of the hesychast

'At the rising and the setting of the sun, withdraw to pray in a quiet and hidden cell and sit on a small stool.'[16] Bend the head towards the knees until there is a slight 'pain in the chest, shoulders and the nape of the neck'. 'In the morning, sit down on a small stool, bring your mind into your heart and keep it there, and as you exert some effort to remain bent over, with pain the chest, shoulders and back of the neck, cry out with great resolve in your spirit or your soul, *Lord Jesus Christ have mercy on me.*'[17]

---

[15] Nicephoros the Solitary, 'Method of Prayer'.

[16] Callistus and Ignatius Xanthopoulos, 'Methode et règle détaillée', *Petite Philocalie de la prière du cœur*, ed. and trans. J. Gouillard, Paris, p. 214.

[17] Gregory of Sinai, *Petite Philocalie de la prière du cœur*, p. 183.

'Remain patiently seated because of him who said *perse-vere in prayer* (Ac 1.14), you will not feel inclined to get up out of negligence because of the sharp pain of the inner invocation of the spirit and the prolonged immobility.'[18] 'Anguish has gripped us, pain like that of a woman in labour' (Jr 6.24).

This ancient technique was sometimes mocked and its practitioners called 'navel gazers'. 'A straight back, a flexible spinal column, are the essential conditions for a wholesome life and a clear conscience. The vertebrae form an axis around which the entire body takes shape, and the importance of this zone on the neuro-vegetative level is essential. Meditation must utilize the back for sitting up straight and arching. Some forms of meditation are not concerned with posture. This is a serious error which the Orthodox monks practising the Jesus prayer committed: bent over with eyes focused on the navel. Does this schizophrenic attitude truly lead to enlightenment or does it fold back on itself in a flight from reality, a return to the umbilical cord? The erect posture of the human being has been the mark of a victory over animality. One can see this evolution by examining the body postures and skeletons of our distant ancestors. And the dignified bearing of statues of the Buddha presents an ideal image of harmonious balance, serene and alert, which we too can attain.'[19]

Olivier Clément gives this bent posture and navel-gazing a completely different interpretation. 'Fixing the gaze on the navel, that is on centre of vitality, is no mere trick in order to concentrate. Rather it means that the entire life force of the person, transforming itself in the awakened heart, must also become offering. *God*, says Gregory Palamas, *can thus receive the desiring part of the soul. God can bring this desire back to its origin*; that is, to an eros for God of which John Climacus speaks. In this way

---

18 Gregory of Sinai, *Petite Philocalie de la prière du cœur*, p. 191.
19 Marc de Smedt, *50 Techniques de méditation*, Retz, 1979, p. 30.

the body also grows attached to God by force of this same desire.'[20]

Similarly, Gregory of Palamas, 'The mind performs exterior acts in a linear movement, as Denys the Areopagite might say. In what the Areopagite calls a circular movement, the mind also returns to itself and accomplishes its deed in itself as it regards itself .... It is what Denys calls a circular movement. It is a most noble act, an act proper to the mind, if there be such a thing. By this act one transcends oneself to unite to God.

'They lie, therefore, and err those who persuade people that it is better to keep the mind out of the body during prayer.... A learned man once wrote that "after the Fall the inner person began to model himself after exterior forms." Henceforth, a person who turned inward would impose on himself a circular and infallible movement instead of a linear movement. Would such a person not profit greatly instead of looking around here and there, occasionally looking down at the chest or navel? In doing this, he imitates the inner movement of his mind and by his posture, he brings into his heart the power of the spirit which spreads beyond. If it is true that the inner beast has its seat of power in the region of the navel or stomach, why not master it while mastering its domain by practising the prayer of the heart?'[21]

'Take care of yourself,' said Moses, 'your entire self. Do not leave without careful vigilance any part of your soul or body. In this way you will break through this area of inferior temptations and present yourself with assurance to the One who scrutinizes the kidneys and the heart, for you will already have done that yourself.'[22]

---

[20] *La Prière de cœur*, Bellefontaine, 1977, p. 96.
[21] Gregory Palamas, *Petite Philocalie*, pp. 203–205.
[22] Gregory Palamas, *Petite Philocalie*, p. 207.

b) The Breath of the Hesychast

'In the beginning the Spirit of God hovered over the waters' (Gn 1.2). *Ruach*, usually translated as 'Spirit', can also be rendered *breath*.

'Yahweh God shaped man from the soil of the ground and blew the breath of life into his nostrils, and man became a living being' (Gn 2.7). Thus the importance of the breath in Hebrew anthropology. Even the notion of Sabbath turns on this theme of breath. The Sabbath is a day when a person, seated before God, stops in order to breathe and, in the breath of God, catches his own.

The hesychasts enter a sort of inner Sabbath, where they sit before God and blend their breath with God's.

John Climacus says, 'May the memory of Jesus be attached to your every breath, then you will know the meaning of stillness',[23] and St Hesychius, 'If you truly wish to be rid of troublesome thoughts, to live in stillness without disruption, to have a vigilant and gentle heart, then let the Jesus prayer become part of your breath.'[24] 'It is necessary to remember God as one breathes. Think of God as often as you breathe.'[25] The whole purpose of this attention to the breath is the re-unification of the whole person so that one might eventually unite one's spirit (breath) with God's Spirit (Breath).

'So that you might keep watch over your breath,' says Isaiah the Anchorite, 'train your untrained spirit that has been pushed around and dissipated by the power of the enemy lest through negligence the enemy returns after baptism with many of his friends (cf Matthew 12.45). When we were purified we received the imprint of the Spirit and the seeds of the Word dwelling within, ... but neglect of the commandments made us fall into the passions and, instead of breathing the Holy Spirit, we were filled with the breath of evil spirits.'[26]

[23] *The Ladder of Divine Ascent*, 27.
[24] *Philocalie des Pères neptiques*, Bellefontaine, 1979, p. 75.
[25] *Philocalie des Pères neptiques*, Bellefontaine, 1979, p. 87.
[26] Gregory of Sinai, *Petite Philocalie*, p. 185.

Nicodemus the Hagorite (1749–1809) continues, 'Why should one hold the breath back during prayer? Because the spirit – in the act of breathing – tends to spill and disperse all over the place. When you say this holy prayer, do not breathe in your usual manner, but gently hold your breath until you have said the Jesus Prayer one time. Then exhale, as the fathers taught.

'– because a measured holding of the breath torments, compresses, and makes the heart work, since it does not receive the air required by nature. The spirit, thanks to this method, remains recollected and can return more easily to the heart thanks both to this effort and pain and the plea-sure which comes to birth from the living and ardent memory of God....

'– because a measured holding of the breath removes hardness and heaviness from the heart, and humid elements of the heart, suitably compressed and warmed up, become as a result more tender, sensitive, humble, more disposed to compunction and more likely to give forth tears. The brain, for its part, also sorts itself out, and at the same time the spirit becomes one with itself, trans-parent, and more capable of union with God which results in supernatural illumination....

'– by this measured retention of the breath, all the other powers of the soul unite and return to the spirit, and by means of the spirit to God. In this way a person offers to God one's entire self, according to Gregory of Thessa-lonica.'[27]

Breath is connected to the heart, which must be conquered and made an acceptable dwelling-place for God. Thus, the hesychasts remain faithful to biblical anthropology and to the invitation of the prophets to return to the heart and change it from a heart of stone into a heart of flesh.

---

[27] See Nicodemus the Hagorite in *Petite Philocalie*.

c) The Importance of the Heart in the Prayer of the Hesychasts

In the Bible, as in the writings of the hesychasts, the heart
is our principle organ, physical and spiritual. It is the
determining principle of every activity and aspiration, the
point from which and towards which all spiritual life
converges. The heart, according to Macarius of Egypt,
houses both justice and iniquity. It is a vase which
contains every vice, but also where one finds God, the
angels, life, the kingdom, light, the apostles, and the treasures of grace.

'When Grace takes possession of the pasture of the
heart, it reigns over all parts of nature, over all thoughts.
For the spirit and all the thoughts of the soul are found in
the heart.' For this reason grace travels with the breath
throughout our entire nature.

'The heart is the depth of a person. In it one finds
knowledge of God as well as our radical dependence on
God and the manifold treasures of the spiritual life. The
word *heart* should not be understood in its ordinary sense
but in the sense of the inner person – according to St Paul
and St Peter, a person hidden in the heart.'[28]

If the Kingdom of God is already within us, as the
Gospel says, where does it reside? The answer is, in the
heart. It does not come from humanity but from the one
who created humanity.

Similarly with grace: 'Macarius says one must look to
see if grace has engraved there the laws of the Spirit. If so,
then where? On the chief organ, the heart, the throne of
grace, there where the spirit and every thought gather.
Now you see the necessity, for those who are dedicated to
the practice of silent vigilance, to bring the spirit back in
the body, especially the body within the body, which we
call the heart.'[29]

---

[28] Theophane the Recluse, *L'Art de la Prière*, p. 262.
[29] Palamas, *Petite Philocalie*, p. 203.

For the hesychasts the heart is inevitably tied to the mind, which one brings into the heart through the breath: 'Seated in the quiet of your cell and gathering together your spirit, make it enter – your spirit – where the breath enters the heart. Push it and force it to remain in the heart with the breath. From the moment it enters the pain and effort will disappear. You will feel joy and grace and all the things that follow. Just as someone who has been away from home a long time rejoices upon returning, reunited with children and spouse, so the spirit, when it reunites with the soul is filled with pleasure and unspeakable joy.'[30]

d) The Descent of the Spirit into the Heart, or the Work of Prayer

According to Bishop Ignace Brianchaninov, the human spirit has a two-fold nature, the heart and the head, which was fragmented after the Fall. The effects of this fragmentation are seen in the mind, which loses contact with the spiritual world, while the blind and impotent heart desperately searches for reality. To rebuild the person in grace is to restore the harmonious rapport between the mind and the heart.

'You've got to get out of your head and into your heart. Right now your thoughts are in your head, and God seems to be outside you. Your prayer and all your spiritual exercises also remain exterior. As long as you are in your head, you will never master your thoughts, which continue to whirl around your head like snow in a winter's storm or like mosquitoes in the summer's heat.'[31]

'If you descend into your heart, you will have no more difficulty. Your mind will empty out and your thoughts will dissipate. Thoughts are always in your mind chasing one another about, and you never quite manage to get

[30] *Philocalie des Pères neptiques*, p. 72.
[31] Theophane the Recluse, *L'Art de la Prière*, p. 252.

them under control. But if you enter into your heart and can remain there, then every time your thoughts invade, you will have only to descend into your heart and your thoughts will vanish into thin air. This will be your safe haven. Don't be lazy! Descend! You will find life in your heart. There you must live.'[32]

'How should one interpret the expression *to concentrate the mind in the heart?* The mind is where one finds one's attention. To concentrate the mind in the heart means to establish the attention in the heart and to see before one, mentally, the invisible God who is always present. That means to turn towards God in praise, the work of grace, and supplication, whilst one keeps watch lest something from outside penetrate within. That is the secret of the spiritual life.'[33]

Symeon the New Theologian reminds us that 'at the beginning the effort to unite the mind and the heart will seem rather dry. We see none of its fruits. The mind in its effort to unite with the heart, encounters straight away an impenetrable darkness, a heart that is hardened by sleep and that does not awaken quickly to compassion.'[34] But with a bit of perseverence, one tastes before long some of the fruits of prayer of the heart: 'Invoked by the prayer of the heart, Christ sends into the heart a spiritual force called peace of Christ, which the mind cannot understand, which words cannot express, and which can only be attained through an experience of grace which is incomprehensible.... What used to require effort and struggle in the earlier phase of practice has become in some sense much easier in this new stage of detachment.... Before the experience of union, the ascetic observed the commandments with a certain difficulty, forcing and straining her fallen being. After the union of mind and heart, the spiritual force which unites the mind to the heart attracts a

---

[32] Theophane the Recluse, *L'Art de la Prière*, p. 252.
[33] Theophane the Recluse, *L'Art de la Prière*, pp. 253–254.
[34] Cited in Simonod, *La Prière de Jésus*, Paris, 1976, p. 46.

person toward the fulfilment of the commandments. It makes one calm, relaxed and full of sweetness as the Psalmist says.'[35]

3. *The Effect of Prayer of the Heart*

a) Affirmation of the Experience and Discernment

'Prayer of the heart has filled me with such happiness that I thought I was no longer on this earth, and I asked myself whether the delights of the Kingdom of Heaven could be any greater than this. This happiness illumined not only my inner soul, but the whole world also appeared beautiful. Everything beckoned me to love and praise God: other people, trees, plants, animals. It all struck me as familiar, and in everything I found the image of the name of Christ. At times I felt so light that I thought I no longer had a body and floated gently in the air. Sometimes I entered entirely within myself. I saw clearly my own heart of hearts and I admired the remarkable creation of the human body. At other times I felt such joy that I thought I had become a king, and in the midst of all these consolations, I wished that God would allow me to die as soon as possible so as to allow my gratitude to overflow at his feet in the spiritual world.'[36]

This happiness of which the pilgrim speaks was the fruit of his prayer. We can read about it in numerous texts from the *Philokalia* with the necessary adaptations, for the domain of 'spiritual sensations' can also become the domain of every illusion.

'Anyone who practises this prayer and omits the language of repentance deludes oneself; for this omission stirs up sentimental love of God, which does nothing other than increase in decadence.'[37]

---

[35] I. Brianchaninov, cited in *La Prière de Jésus*, p. 47.
[36] *The Way of a Pilgrim.*
[37] I. Brianchaninov, cited in *La Prière de Jésus*, p. 39.

'There can be no doubt that when the mind is influenced by divine light it becomes completely transparent to the point of seeing its own light. This occurs when the power of the soul becomes master of the passions. But everything which presents itself to the mind under any form whatever, light or fire, comes from the machinations of the evil one.

'St Paul teaches quite clearly when he says that "Satan disguises himself as an angel of light" (2 Co 11, 14). Let no one, then embrace the ascetical life motivatd by a hope of this sort.... For the goal is to arrive at the intimate love of God and fullness of heart.'[38]

The affirmation of experience and discernment are two constants in these texts. The effects of prayer vary according to the level of purification and the simplicity of heart that one has attained. Thus Theophane the Recluse can very nearly build a ladder of these different effects.

'At first prayer is extraordinarily pure, from which grows a warmth in the heart, then a strange and holy energy. Afterwards come divine tears and the peace they contain, and from one's thoughts burst forth the purification of the mind and the contemplation of divine mysteries. 'Finally, the heart silently flares up and is illumined.'[39]

This search for immediate experience is the overriding concern of the entire hesychastic tradition. The feeling of fullness and certitude, so vigorously affirmed by Macarius and Diadochus, will haunt a significant portion of the Byzantine tradition. For Symeon the New Theologian there is only a conscious indwelling of the Holy Spirit in the heart. 'Have no doubt that Christ shows himself according to what he himself said to those who keep his commandments, and by this manifestation, the Holy Spirit is communicated to them. Finally both the Spirit and the Father dwell inseparably with them. People no longer speak of these things from their own experience.

[38] Diadochus of Photiki, *Petite Philocalie*, p. 61.
[39] *Petite Philocalie*, p. 25.

'You have therefore learnt, my dear one, that the kingdom of God is within you, and all eternal riches are at hand. So try to see and receive and acquire these treasures. But in congratulating yourself on possessing them do not expose yourself to the risk of losing them entirely. Cry, prostrate yourself like the blind man and say: "Have mercy on me, Son of God, and open the eyes of my soul so that I might see the light of this world, which is you, who are God, and that I too might become a child of the light. Do not leave me unworthy to share in your divinity, O Gracious God. Show yourself to me that I may know that you have loved me, Lord, for having kept your divine commandments. Send me also, God of Mercy, your Paraclete, that I may be instructed in knowledge of you and be told of your hidden ways, O Lord of all. Shine forth upon me true light, O God rich in mercy, so that I may see your glory, the glory that you had, together with the Father, before the world was. Dwell in me, as you have said, so that I too might become worthy of dwelling in you and of entering incessantly in you and taking constant possession of you. Deign, O Hidden One, to take form in me, so that, gazing upon your unfathomable beauty, I might bear your image, you who are beyond the heavens, and forget all things visible. Give me the glory which you gave your Father, so that I might become with your grace like you, God, and be ever with you for all eternity. Amen."'[40]

b) Fire and Tears

'Warmth is born of prayer of the heart. It is written, *My heart burns within me* and in my meditation a fire leapt up (Ps 39.3). It is the fire that Christ came to throw upon the earth of our hearts, which in the past was controlled by thorns of passions. But now, our hearts are under the dominion of grace. Christ himself said, *I have come to cast*

---

[40] Symeon the New Theologian.

fire upon the earth and how I wish it were blazing already (Lk 12.49).

'It is the fire which blazed in Cleopas and his companion, warming them as it made them exclaim almost in ecstasy to one another, *were not our hearts burning while he spoke to us along the road'* (Lk 24.32).

'From this warmth which comes from the grace of contemplation is born a stream of tears. From these continuous tears, the soul receives peaceful thoughts and ascends to the purity of the mind. And through the mind's purity, one begins to see the mysteries of God.'[41]

For the hesychasts, as for Bernanos, evil is the cold. God is the interior Sun who melts the heart.

c) Silence and Tranquillity

Warmth and tears purify the heart and prepare it for the vision of God in silence of heart. This silence, empty of all thought, is one of the conditions for and effects of that tranquillity which the monk seeks.

'When you are aware that the sweetness of divine grace is working in you, and when prayer opens up your heart, you really should remain right there. Do not interrupt it. Do not get up to chant psalms when God is determined to continue this work in you. For to do this would be to leave God who is in your own depths in order to look for God on the mere surface of things, as if one should depart the lofty heights for the flatness of the plain. You would only be chasing away prayer and depriving the mind of silence at the very moment when inner peace (*hesychia*), in the strict sense, requires the mind to be kept in the peace and calm of silence.

'God is peace and a stranger to noise and agitation. Moreover, when you are deep in interior prayer, do not give in to the temptation to let fantasies and visions enter

---

[41] Callistus and Ignatius Xanthopoulos, *Philocalie des Pères neptiques*, p. 134.

in; for such daydreaming and tyrannical movements do not cease automatically when the mind enters the heart to pray. Only those who resist and conquer these distracting thoughts, who attach themselves with a firm heart to Jesus Christ attain the overflowing grace of the Holy Spirit.'[42]

'It is especially important to try to render the mind deaf and dumb during the time of prayer, keeping the heart silent and free from every thought, whatever it might be, even if it is a good thought.'[43]

d) Incessant Prayer

The most important 'effect' of prayer of the heart is the passage from *doing* to *being*. The time comes when the hesychast *becomes* prayer, a state of uninterrupted silence, peace and communion with God. The invocation becomes one with the beating of the heart. 'When the Spirit dwells within one, one can no longer cease praying; for the Spirit does not cease praying in the person. Whether asleep or awake prayer is always present in the soul. While drinking, eating, sleeping, relaxing, the perfume of prayer exudes from the soul. From now on, one no longer prays at determined times; one is always praying. The movements of the purified mind are like muted voices which sing psalms in hiddenness to the ineffable'.[44]

The Russian Pilgrim echoes Isaac of Nineveh, 'I grew so accustomed to prayer of the heart that I unceasingly practised it and finally felt that the prayer prayed itself without any activity on my part. It started up in my mind and heart whether I was awake or asleep and never let up so much as for one second'.[45]

---

[42] Nil Sorsky, in G. Maloney, *La Spiritualité de Nil Sorsky*, Bellefontaine, 1978, p. 144.

[43] I. Hausherr, *Les Leçons d'un contemplatif. Le traité d'Evagre le Pontique*, Beauchesne, Paris, 1960. See Evagrius, *Chapters on Prayer*, 11.

[44] *Petite Philocalie*, p. 82.

[45] *The Way of a Pilgrim*.

e) Charity

The entrance into the uninterrupted state of prayer is not an entrance into a second state. At the prompting of the Holy Spirit, the heart identifies itself more and more with the heart of Christ and becomes capable of universal love.

Under the effects of the Holy Spirit the Christian becomes reconciled with everything and everyone, thanks to a peculiar meditation at once humble and profoundly spiritual. The Christian begins to feel compassion for all humanity and for each person in particular. This compassion is transformed into love.'[46]

'Without prayer all the virtues are like trees without soil. Prayer is the soil that allows all the virtues to grow.... The follower of Christ must live for Christ alone. When the Christian does this, she will love unfailingly all God's creatures. People think you have to start by loving others and then love God. I did too. But it is of no use. When, however, I began by loving God, I discovered my neighbour in this love. And in this love of God, even my enemies became my friends, divine creatures.'[47]

Isaac the Syrian says, 'When does one realize that one has attained purity? When one considers all people as good, when no one strikes you as impure or tarnished. Then one truly is pure in heart.'

In the most sublime states of prayer, one does not speak of others going to hell, only oneself – like the cobbler of Alexandria who prayed (according to St Anthony) that all might be saved and that he alone would merit perdition. Similarly, Symeon the New Theologian regarded all his companions as saints and himself as the only sinner. On Judgement Day, he believed, all would be saved. He alone would be cut off.

---

[46] See I. Brianchaninov cited in Simonod, *La Prière de Jésus*, p. 44.
[47] Archimandrite Spiridon, *Mes missions en Sibérie*, Paris, pp. 43–44.

Conclusions

The hesychasts believed that a person is created to become one with God in heart, mind, soul and body. This body-spirit is not a particular faculty but the centre where all the faculties unite, where one is gathered together, transcends oneself and where is inscribed one's personal vocation.

The West, marked by a sort of implicit Platonism, has a tendency to unite spirit to Spirit, mistaking the body as an obstacle to authentic 'spiritual life'. In reality, it is the whole person who receives grace. Hence, the hesychast's warnings against purely physical visions or imaginary visions.

The anthropology of hesychasm emphasizes the two basic rhythms of our existence as embodied spirits, the breath and the heart.

The rhythm of the breath is the only one which we can control, not in order to conquer it but in order to make an offering of it. It determines how we will live from moment to moment, speeding up or slowing down; it closes us in on ourselves or opens us up to transcendence.

Moreover, the technical aspect of this prayer is neither mistaken nor idolized. Without doubt the most characteristic trait of hesychasm and the most precious legacy bequeathed to Christianity is this indissoluable union of the mental and the physical, and the ascetic practice and rigour it demands, with the highest mistrust of all devices and techniques in the mystery of the soul's union with God.[48]

[48] See A. Bloom, in *Études carmélitaines*, 1949.

Chapter Nine

Praying with all the Senses

'God is spirit, and those who worship must worship in spirit and truth' (Jn 4.24). Do not these words of Jesus contradict the conclusions of the previous chapter? It depends how we translate the Greek of the New Testament, *patri en pneumati kai aletheia*.

To pray in spirit, *en pneumati*, does not mean to close the doors of physical perception. On the contrary, it means to open them, to introduce *pneuma*, breath, to each of the senses, that they might become organs of knowledge of God. This is what the Fathers of the Church understood when they developed the doctrine of the spiritual senses, inhabited and animated by the Spirit of God. Christianity does not view the human being as Plato said, 'the tomb of the soul', but as St Paul said, 'the temple of the Holy Spirit'.

Origen, and after him Gregory of Nyssa, Macarius, Diadochus of Photiki, Maximus the Confessor, Symeon the New Theologian, proposed a theory of the spiritual senses which was tied to the sacramental life. We move through the domain of the senses towards the Kingdom which is *beyond the senses*. It is to go from those things which pass away toward that which never passes away. The senses are not destroyed but spiritualized, transfigured. They become, as it were, divine senses which render a person ever more *capax dei* – a capacity for God.

In his book, *Contra Celsum*, Origen says, 'consideration

of this question will, following the words of Scripture, yield the conclusion that there is a certain divine sense which the blessed find present. In the words of Solomon, *you will find a divine sense.* And this sense includes various forms: vision, which can see realities that are not bodily, like the cherubim and seraphim; hearing, which attends to sounds that do not pass through the air; taste, in order to savour the bread come down from heaven which gives life to the world; smell, which perceives the perfumes described by Paul as, *the good odour of Christ*; touch, thanks to which John claims to have touched with his hands the Word of Life. Having discovered this divine sense, the holy prophets saw divinely, listened divinely, tasted and smelt in the same way, by means of a sense which is not sensible, so to speak. And they touched the Logos by means of faith, as though it were an emanation that came to them from afar to heal them. Thus they saw what they claim to have seen; they understood what they said they understood. They experience sensations of the same order when they ate the scroll of a book which was given to them.'[1]

For Origen, the God who lives in inaccessible light can in some sense be grasped by the senses and not only by the heart and the intellect, because God truly became incarnate in Jesus Christ. As Irenaeus says, 'Jesus is the visible aspect of the invisible.' No one has seen or ever will see God in Himself. God can only be grasped or comprehended in creation or in His humanity.

Christ becomes the object of each of the soul's senses. Christ calls himself the true light that illumines the eyes of the soul, the word to be heard, the bread to be tasted. In the same way Christ is called the oil of anointing, so that the soul might delight in the fragrance of the Word. The Word became flesh, tangible and graspable, so that we might grasp the Word of Life.[2]

---

[1] *Contra Celsum*, I, 48.
[2] See Origen, *Commentary on the Song of Songs*, II.

To Meditate and Pray with all the Senses

In prayer, the Spirit heals before it illuminates. A person learns to see, hear, touch, smell, taste *what is* and only then to enter into the presence of the *One who is*.

The meditative use of all the senses can thus be the beginning of profound prayer. It is a question of considering them allies in prayer and not enemies or obstacles to grace. Everything which is known is known in the body. Paul Evdokimov, following the Orthodox tradition, speaks of a 'sense for God', the participation of one's entire being in prayer.

One remembers only what one has felt in one's body. In ancient tradition, to remember God is not a mere act of the intelligence; it is to preserve in oneself the seal of a presence. *Walk in my presence and be perfect*, said God to Abraham.

To pray is not to think about God but to discern the enveloping presence that guides us. This discernment cannot be reduced to a feeling. This presence completely exceeds our perception but nevertheless it truly communicates something of itself in accord with our ever expanding capacity to receive. To borrow a distinction made by Gregory of Palamas, God's *essence* remains inaccessible, but His *energy* is discernible through the senses. We are not in the sun, and yet the sun is the source of each ray of light. To pray is to allow oneself to be exposed to the sun.

Ascetic practice begins with the purification of the senses. It is a matter of letting them grow accustomed to the presence of God, of teaching them silence, without the mind's interpretations, leaving them naked in the embrace with the One who is.

Listen

Hear, oh Israel ... you will love ... The first command is *listen*. Prayer, in fact, is not talking to God but being quiet in order to listen. The first thing one discovers is not God's infinite silence but the noise of one's own thoughts, the concepts which humanity has forged throughout the centuries. Listen to the noise, the clamour, whether great or small, the words which we use even when saying something about God. But God is not a concept but someone whose presence resounds in us and comes to birth in powerful and suggestive echoes of Presence.

Listen! Open your ears! It is often said that Israel is a people who listen rather than see (like the Greeks). But why honour one sense over another or for that matter pray with one of the senses rather than another? Isn't there a comprehensive sort of listening which is also a comprehensive attention?

It is true that in the desert there is nothing to see. The eyes adjust poorly to the light, but there is the song of the sands, trembling souls, voices in the wind, and the inner word, *Hear, oh Israel!*

The people who bear God's word are the people who listen. To pray is to listen. Simply to bend one's ear and occasionally resist the desire to make immediate sense of everything so that the silence might be able to increase in us a higher desire. But the One Who Speaks to us never says a word. To listen quietens us down, and in this silence we come to understand to what extent the Other is the completely Other.

See

'Before, I knew you only by hearsay but now, having seen you with my own eyes, I retract what I have said, and repent in dust and ashes' (Jb 42.5).

To hear someone is not the same as seeing. Human desire is also a desire to see, and if we desire God, we desire to see God – as He is, and not just as we imagine Him to be: 'We are well aware that when he appears we shall be like him, because we shall see him as he really is' (1 Jn 3.2).

In order to see God 'as he really is', both the eye and the

ear need purification. If not there is every likelihood of seeing nothing but a mirage, a projection. Anyone who has truly seen a rose 'as it really is' knows what it is to pray. A rose or a face. Where others saw an adulterer or a sinner, Jesus saw a woman. His vision did not stop at the mask of a stern look. He contemplated her face. To pray is to contemplate the face of all things, the presence of this face and the intimate exchange which makes it a sign of God's tenderness. One is always beautiful in the eyes of someone who prays.

If our eyes really began to see what was before them; if our vision took the time to settle down and rest in what it saw, it would also discover that everything is looking at us, that everything is praying. Stop labelling everything. Move from observation to contemplation. This is the movement of the prayer of vision. See the invisible through the visible. Move towards that inaccessible point where all vision meets. Seeing becomes vision and vision union. We shall become like God because we shall see God as He is.

Touch

We see and hear from a distance, but the Presence only grips us through the sense of touch. Moreover, it is the progression indicated by St John as if the use of each sense showed a degree of particular intimacy with the Word of Life: 'Something which has existed since the beginning, which we have heard, which we have seen with our own eyes, which we have watched and touched with our own hands, the Word of life – this is our theme. That life was made visible; we saw it and are giving our testimony ...' (1 Jn 1–2).

That which we hear, see, touch, says St John, *is what has existed since the beginning*. There is nothing to add, nothing to devise. It is a matter of applying our senses to what already is so that it might show itself.

Touch can be frightening. It is 'thicker' than hearing or

seeing, more attached to the material, the heaviness of things.

In prayer, we grow accustomed to hearing the inaudible, to seeing the invisible, to what is intangible. Recall the experience of Teilhard de Chardin holding a piece of metal. This was his first 'feeling of God'. The infinite made itself present in this minute particle of the universe.

'If you but knew how deep the skin was,' said Paul Valéry. But, it depends on how you touch it. There are some who touch you as though you were a cactus and others who would squeeze the juice out of you. There are hands which flatten you, which make an object out of you, and there are hands which calm, heal and sometimes even divinize you (think of the imposition of hands for both healing and the communication of grace).

The ancients often speak of work as the prayer of hands. But do hands pray *only* when they work? Can they not also pray while caressing, that is, when suffused by love and respect, when spiritualized?

The prayer of touching is the prayer of the body which does not cling, which does not wrap itself around someone else. To touch God or to let oneself be touched by Him is to feel enveloped by space. God never smothers us. Prayer is an embrace that liberates. One does not pray with clenched fists or claws, or with grit under one's fingernails, but with open hands, with palms open.

Taste

Through hearing, sight and touch the Presence has become something familiar. Can we take a step closer? The Psalms invite us *to taste and see the goodness of the Lord*.

To pray is to have a taste for God. *Let him kiss me with the kisses of his mouth*, says the first line of the Song of Songs. It is not enough to hear God's commandment. One must also see it incarnated in a person of justice and then taste it, appreciate for itself, reveal it in one's life.

Rabbi Isaac asks, 'Why doesn't Scripture say, "let him

love me" instead of "let him give me a kiss"?'[3] Through kissing, lovers exchange spirits (their breath) and that is why a kiss is placed on the mouth, the source of spirit (*pneuma*). When the spirits of two lovers meet through a kiss, mouth to mouth, their spirits are never again separated. After this to die by a kiss would be most desirable, the soul receives a kiss from the Lord, and by this she is united to the Holy Spirit never again to be separated. This is why the assembly of Israel says: 'Let him give me a kiss from his mouth so that our spirit might unite to His and never again be separated.' The Fathers of the Church, following the rabbis, take up these themes of taste and the mystical kiss in the context of the Eucharist.

A sacrament is the visible sign of an invisible reality. As a mother's kiss is the visible sign of her love, so the Eucharist is the visible sign of God's love for us. God becomes our bread and wine and wants to be tasted, known interiorly.

One is aware of body's response to a kiss on the lips and the quivers it excites. Prayer that one can taste is an entrance into the nuptial chamber, the mystery of the union of created and uncreated. Thus God is experienced, like Augustine says, as closer to me than I am to myself.

Smell

After an embrace, the body of another leaves a scent. Once again the metaphor of love seems more adequate than a more cerebral metaphor to describe the lived experience of prayer. *My love is a sachet of myrrh lying between my breasts* (Cant. 1.13). There is no lovelier image to describe the loftiest heights of the prayer of the heart. The presence of God impregnates us, then, within and without, and all our actions are like the perfumed scent of Christ living in us.

The Song of Songs (1.12) has this metaphor, *While the*

---

3   *The Zohar* II, 124 b.

king rests in his own room my nard yields its perfume. The Zohar interprets it like this. 'The king is the Holy One, blessed be He. *In his own room* means the person who is attached to the Lord and walking the narrow path, the person in whom the Lord takes up residence. *My nard yields its perfume* refers to the good works achieved by a person.'[4]

The sense of smell is perhaps our most subtle sense but also perhaps our most feared, if the success of deodorants is any indication. One's scent is, in a sense, one's own secret, one's essence.

In the world of prayer, the phenomenon of spiritual perfume is not rare. St Seraphim of Sarov introduced his friend Motovilov to prayer not only by his own deep peace and gentleness, but also through scent.[5]

Moreover, no tradition overlooks the power of incense. Its role is truly to make us enter a new dimension of awareness, to awaken us to the beauty of Divine Presence. So one can cease wanting to hear anything. Close your eyes and simply breathe. With each inhalation feel the Presence of the Living One spread throughout all our members.

The spread of this incense also symbolizes the act by which one gives oneself entirely to God in prayer. It is the act of love *par excellence*. One thinks also of Mary Magdalene at the feet of Jesus.

When we pray with the Psalmist, *May my prayer be like incense in your presence* (Ps 141), we wish to give ourselves totally to God. Henceforth everything belongs to God, as a grain of incense belongs to the burning coal.

The Liturgy or the Unification of all the Senses

We have read too much John of the Cross not to distrust our senses in prayer. To pray does not mean to look for

[4]   *The Zohar* I, 56 b.
[5]   See V. Lossky, *Théologie mystique de l'Église d'Orient*, Paris, 1944, pp. 226–227.

sensations nor to take pleasure in them. Rather, one learns to discern between them, to distinguish the godly, the natural or the demonic. The godly sensations are ones we can make use of in prayer: directing them to God and going ourselves towards God with all our being. The natural ones can be used in meditation. It is only the diabolical ones which reduce us to a sterile and schizoid narcissism and cut us off from Reality. We are stuck in a meaningless flow of sensations which we take for reality. Making an absolute of a relative is a form of idolatry.

A sensation, then, can be an icon, an image or an idol. It is an icon when it brings us into the presence of God, an image when it reveals the beauty of an object and an idol when it tempts us to mistake an image for Reality.

In ancient tradition the liturgy, which is the place of communal prayer, was also considered the place of purification and unification of all the senses. Hearing is addressed by singing, sight by icons and light, touch by posture, movement and reverencing of icons, taste by the Eucharist, and smell by incense.

No sense should be deprived of its role in prayer, for it is the whole person who must enter into the presence of God, and the liturgy is the prayer of all the senses. One can sing with St Augustine, 'Late have I loved you, oh Beauty ever ancient, ever new; late have I loved you.... You were within me, yet I was outside myself. You were with me, but I was not with you.... You have called me; you have cried out and shattered my deafness. You have shown me your light, and your brightness has chased away my blindness. You have exuded your perfume. I breathed it in and now I pant after you. I tasted you and now I hunger and thirst for you. You have touched me and now I burn for your peace.'[6]

6   *Confessions*, X, 27.